LIVING LIFE /FORWARD

LIVING LIFE /FORWARD
Discovering the Power of Supernatural Upgrade

Troy A Brewer

Aventine Press

Published by Aventine Press
55 East Emerson St.
Chula Vista CA, 92101
www.aventinepress.com

ISBN: 978-1-59330-821-6
Library of Congress Control Number: 2013907999
Library of Congress Cataloging-in-Publication Data
Living Life /Forward/ Troy Brewer

Printed in the United States of America

I dedicate this book to my four children. Maegan, Benjamin, Luke and Rhema. You have blessed me and added richness to my life that is beyond my simple vocabulary. The fantastic four of the Brewer bunch are all people who I know will go deeper and higher into that undiscovered place that is way past where your Daddy has ever been.

You are also people I am happy to have as friends.

Ya'll rock and I dedicate this book to you in supernatural hope of your heritage and better things to come.

Go get 'em kids.

TABLE OF CONTENTS

Introduction

THE NEED FOR UPGRADE

Of the increase of his government and peace there shall be no end...

Isaiah 9:7

A funny thing happened at an airport with me several years ago. With an hour left to go before my flight back to the United States, I sat thinking about the first food I would eat on blessed Texas ground.

As my mind lined up a mental buffet of Hotdogs, Bar-B-Que and Tex-Mex...the Holy Spirit crashed my cart with an unexpected God thought.

I knew it was the Lord and I knew if I responded quickly, exactly what He put on my heart would happen. So before I let my head talk me out of a blessing, I stepped up to the counter and said, "Ma'am if you have any unclaimed upgrades laying around, I would like to pick one up please."

Now I did this with my best *Texas charm* and hick accent, but it wasn't my old flair that was working, -it was the Lord.

That flight home from Central America was my first time in first class. It gave me nearly five hours to contemplate and wonder how many unclaimed upgrades I have laying around.

The first thing I did when I got back was put pen to paper and get very intentional about learning about the Kingdom subject of upgrade and progression.

Since that day, I have been passionate about developing skills at the art of upgrade. This study has become a big part of my life long lesson of learning because all of us need to go to the next level. The next level is messing with us and daring us to come /forward.

The only reason this book interests you at all is because there is something in you too, that wants to get really good at getting better. I love that and I would bet big God likes that too.

Here are some Crazy thoughts on God and His connection to your next upgrade.

CREATED TO UPGRADE
I have come to find out that my upgrade is also His upgrade. I mean to say it doesn't just belong to me. I have learned that our calling to move /forward and progress is a big part of His story as the Creator. He has made sure there is more out there right now and there will be even more out there again tomorrow because He is counting on you to go after it.

I couldn't help but notice God prewired the universe to continue to create and expand. Never stopping, always moving /forward and here's the thing that really makes my heart beat, -you and I are the greatest part of that creation.

You are His creation and you must move /forward from here. You didn't used to be His creation, you still are, and all of His creation is designed to move /forward. You will not be happy staying where you are, the way you are. Everything is not yet created in your life.

Furthermore, God didn't used to be the Creator. He is still the most creative person in the universe. For God to stop creating would be like Eddie Van Halen hanging up his guitar or Thomas

Kincade deciding he is no longer an artist. The Creator is who He is.

He is still creating and you are still an unfinished product of His wonderful heart towards you. That's why He made you a creature of hope, a pursuer and dreamer. He made you to long for an upgrade.

The fact of the matter is that He longs for your upgrade. That is God's heart and He wants you to know His heart. You might as well be willing to want to know what God thinks, otherwise you will never be able to be in agreement with Him.

You were built to move /forward and transform into something altogether wonderful. You are a magnificent work in progress learning to look much more like your destiny, than your history. Think about that and go ahead and say "Wow!"

UPGRADE IS A "GOOD" THING
From a created earth with endless possibilities, God created us and coded our DNA, just like the universe, to be people attracted to the next level and generally happy with anything related to improvement.

At each unfinished stage, God announces His goodness over you the way He did at the end of every day in the Genesis story. When He sees you complete one small step towards something better, at the end of that day He declares it monumental and says,

"...it is good."
Genesis 1:21

Yes, <u>your</u> universe is still expanding. So why would we dare think it's ok to not progress & go /Forward?

On He goes, naturally and supernaturally, creating wonderful things for us to step up into. But what He prepares for us has to be pursued and partnered with. That's why He made one of His highest honors to be crowned upon those who are willing to go after it.

It is the glory of God to conceal a thing: but the honor of kings is to search out a matter.
Proverbs 25:2

He is patient and loving, confident and trusting that we will reach our highest potential. It is His *glory* to conceal it and our *honor* to go after it.

TIME TO MOVE /FORWARD
I want to tell you it is not treason to search out the endless heart of this Creator and to go after Him. You are not stupid for wanting better things.

There are promises in need of adoption, innovation and ideas desperate to be discovered. There are dreams to be realized and passions to be pursued. Vision is exploding anew to be mapped out and legacy is being permanently laid down. I think God wants you and I to be neck deep in it.

BEING CAREFUL
All of us think sometimes God doesn't care about your upgrade but let me tell you what He really doesn't care about. He doesn't care if it takes a long time for us to find the things and the identity He has already put out there for us. Because He didn't create it all to be found at once. He loves the time we spend with Him in the process of Upgrade.

That's why He gave us time, so that everything didn't happen at once, and time also provided a safe place for a redemptive work.

A place outside of eternity where things in the present could be buried in our past.

IN YOU GOD TRUSTS
No matter how hard He worked on it, and no matter how magnificent, He just trusts that we will go after it. He made it for us to discover it. He also made it so that it can only be found if we are willing to go after it. We must partner with His heart and His passion to find it. We must become interested in our upgrade.

So what are we waiting for?

Like a super proud Papa hiding Easter eggs in plain sight for His infant to stumble upon, His joy is for us to find what He has made for us to discover.

See, in pursuing Him as our life, we find life undiscovered.

There are still Niagara falls in your life which you have never seen that are closer than you ever could envision. You don't know that there are magnificent redwoods in one part of your journey that you have never imagined you could walk under and great coral reefs with colors you never comprehended. But these things are not where you are at. They are /forward and they must be lived out.

You are not too old, nor do you have too much history to discover the jaw dropping wonder of what God still has for you. You just have to reignite the supernatural, God given, fire for what is out there and in there.

There is a you out there, no one has yet seen. A life out there, you have not yet lived and an ongoing call to take another step toward it. You must move /forward. You've got to get your upgrade.

A FEVER FOR /FORWARD

Anyone who gets close to God begins to get the fever for /forward. There will be a whole chapter on this later. I've got it. I've got it bad.

I have been in constant transition since the day I got saved in May of 86. The church I have pastored since 1995 has never looked the same from one year to the next. I have learned that the messiness of transition and the joy of discovery is normal for people who choose not to live a powerless life.

I have also learned that it doesn't set well with a big part of all of us. The need for security and fear of survival is in direct contradiction of the fever for /forward.

Like my friend Dave Crone, who maps out his life message in his amazing book, I have found a big part of mine.

The Scottish clan Douglas has passed down a prophetic legacy in form of a 700 year old family motto and guess what it is...

"/Forward"

One word that takes an eternity to discover. It speaks of motivation and promise. Relentless pursuit and perseverance. Transition, hope and pioneering. I love that word.

Far better than my family's motto whose name is Brewer and probably has something to do with a beer drinking, trouble maker, I have adopted the motto of /forward and so titled this book.

See, in hanging around Jesus, I have learned to fight for greatness. In learning the fear of the Lord, which is to love what He loves and to hate what He hates, I have grown to hate settling down for easier when I can have better. Easier is rarely, if ever, better.

My fever for /forward is contagious. I am praying I infect you and every reader with the bug for better.

Over the years I have contemplated better and /forward. This book is a collection of thoughts, experiences and how we get our Kingdom upgrades.

It's what Aslan, The Lion of Narnia, calls going higher and deeper, because the inside is much larger than the outside.

So put on your thinking hat, take a hit from your dreaming pipe and get ready for an upgrade. Things are about to go way up for you.
/Forward -Forever.
Troy

GOD THOUGHTS AND MEDITATIONS
SUMMARY OF INTRODUCTION

There is an endless discovery of what God governs over and what He rules with His peace.
Of the increase of his government and peace there shall be no end... Isaiah 9:7

God is still in the creating business and right now He is creating things for you to discover, things only you can discover.

The Genesis story tells us God celebrates progress and calls it good at each incremental step. He didn't wait until it was perfectly completed to call it good. He called the end of every day "good."

There is a great honor in the willingness to discover.
It is the glory of God to conceal a thing: but the honor of kings is to search out a matter.   Proverbs 25:2

Memorable quote
"I have learned that the messiness of transition and the joy of discovery is normal for people who choose not to live a powerless life."

"When we pursue Jesus as our life, we find life undiscovered."

Jesus replied, *"What is impossible with men
is possible with God."*
Luke 18:27

Why set we here until we die?
2 Kings 7:3

SECTION ONE
THE FIGHT FOR /FORWARD

Johnny Ringo: "Don't any of ya have the guts to play for blood?"

Doc Holiday : "I'm your huckleberry."
— Tombstone

"None of you understand. I'm not locked up in here with you.
You're locked up in here with me."
— Watchmen

Stephen: "Fine speech. Now what do we do?"
William Wallace: "Just be yourselves."
Hamish: "Where are you going?"
William Wallace: "I'm going to pick a fight."
Hamish: "Well, we didn't get dressed up for nothing."
— Braveheart

CHAPTER ONE

The Fight for Greatness

Let's talk about things worth fighting for. Not everything is worth fighting over, but greatness...that's something worth a good old fashioned throw-down.

Anyone who begins to hang out with Jesus, no matter what kind of history they have, begins to contemplate their own untapped greatness. After a while in His presence, you become willing to fight for it.

The dirty dozen whom Jesus assembled, were men of no notoriety before Jesus joined them. Yet, there was something about His presence that made them all feel like they were God's favorite and could do anything.

Luke 9:46

Then there arose a reasoning among them, which of them should be greatest.

Luke 22:24

And there was also a strife among them, which of them should be accounted the greatest.

Matthew 18:1

At the same time came the disciples unto Jesus, saying, Who is the greatest in the kingdom of heaven?

Mark 9:34

But they held their peace: for by the way they had disputed among themselves, who should be the greatest.

Hanging around Jesus Christ, breathing His words of life and thinking his thoughts makes you want to fight for greatness. So why isn't there more of that?

I am afraid a lot of Christianity doesn't have much to do with Jesus. A lot of the works of our churches might have nothing to do with His heart.

Don't worry this isn't going to be another church bashing book. The church is messed up because we Christians are messed up. It's not the other way around. It's a fact that sometimes Christians have to be reached by Jesus Himself.

Sadly, a lot of Christianity is more famous for dregs than for the best wine at the marriage supper. Here in the geographical *bible noose* of the southern United States, the clarion call has been more of a shout "You had better not" rather than "Go forth."

I am starting to see that change.

RELIGION'S RED LIGHT
Religion trains us to think the worst thing that can happen is to do something wrong. While Jesus teaches the worst thing that can happen, is for you to do nothing at all! You are going to have to fight through this.

In Matthew 25, Jesus tells a story about a man who was afraid to do what his master had commissioned him to do. Instead of taking the master's coin to the marketplace and gaining more, he simply did nothing and gave his master back the single coin. The response is shocking.

'You wicked and lazy servant,.... you ought to have deposited my money with the bankers, and at my coming I would have received back my own with interest...take the (coin) from him... And cast the unprofitable servant into the outer darkness. There will be weeping and gnashing of teeth.'
Matthew 25:14-30

Apparently, God takes advancement and multiplication very seriously. In this parable His wrath is displayed, not at the mistakes we make in moving /forward, but in the mistake of refusing to move at all. Don't miss this point.

The disciples knew this from living with Jesus. That's why they didn't fight over what the right steps to be great were, they knew there was grace for those kinds of things. They fought over who would be the greatest.

When we are afraid we are going to mess up, we refuse to move /forward. If the enemy can convince us we are going to get in bad trouble if we don't do everything perfect, well...it's a huge win for hell.

The devil would much rather have us cowering in a corner like the church is Joan Crawford from *"Mommy Dearest."* People who are convinced they are messed up, are always going to mess up. We need to be healed of that mess.

Our Dad is more like Atticus Finch from *To Kill a Mockingbird*, Daddy Warbucks from *Annie* and Chris Gardner from *The Pursuit of Happiness*. From these types of identities we are unafraid to just plain live life and to live it to the fullest.

You are encouraged and empowered to continuously do great things and live life greatly when you know you are in good standing with an amazing father. You are.

BABY STEPS

In 2011, I was teaching at a conference in the mountains west of Managua, Nicaragua. I heard my good friend, Steve Fish say something amazing as he taught on the gift of prophecy.

He said that under the old covenant you had to get everything right or you could never be prophetic but things are very different under the new covenant.

Now, he can teach it a lot better than I can, but the point he was making is that when you are in relationship with God as your Father, there is room to stumble when you are learning how to walk.

"When my kids were taking their first steps and they fell after only moving an inch, "Steve said, "I didn't scold them and say we don't fall down in this house! No, I clapped and celebrated and shouted, Look at him taking steps. He's moving /forward, that's amazing!"

In so doing, his kids learned how to walk and even run. All of us learned how to walk because we had not yet learned to fear failing. We were uncoordinated, we didn't know what we were doing, we weren't sure of the outcome or even how to take the next step. We just went for it and our parents clapped, so we did it again. Somehow it was perfect.

The point is not that you fell when you were trying to walk. The point is that you were actually doing it. A good dad celebrates when you fight for steps /forward and so does your Father in heaven.

/FORWARD IN THE FRAY

For most of us, not only does the act of moving /forward look like a train wreck, but so do the circumstance in which we are stumbling through.

It is hard to believe that God is happy with you when you are stumbling in a place that doesn't honor or glorify the Lord.

God says move /forward and I will celebrate your progression. He does not say, clean the place up and get your act together before you do.

When Your Daddy gives you a great big ice cream cone, He is not saying do not make a mess. He is giving you a green light to go for it.

He already knows there will be a mess and He is confident he can handle the cleanup.

If you fear the mess will bring His disapproval, you will never take your first bite, even though he has purchased and handed it to you. This is where a lot of us are today.

STEPS IN A MESS

Just ten miles south of Texas is the trash dumps of Matamoros Mexico. It is the ugliest place I have seen and the most despicable environment I have ever witnessed. I have loved on people living in trash dumps in several different countries but there was something especially terrible about this one.

Inside this disgusting arena of waste and hopelessness, were hundreds of beautiful families with sometimes thousands of little kids. Most of them were enslaved by the local *mafioso* for owing them money. Unable to pay the high interests of their loans, they were imprisoned as slaves.

For 15 years, we partnered with Mission Divina church in Brownsville and made over 100 trips of relief to these people. It was on one of the first of these trips, I saw something that changed my life.

It was hot and when it is hot there, the dump is especially brutal. I can't even describe the smell and the fumes of this place. But there we were, and there was a line of several hundred people waiting patiently for a box of groceries. My wife and I were dispersing cold water bottles and handing out little toys to kids in the line.

All of a sudden, a large group of smiling people began to applaud and shout. I turned to see what they were celebrating and there in the trash was an infant boy taking his very first steps towards his Papa.

He was filthy. He had no shoes and no shirt. His mama, was a girl that looked no older than 16. The ground he was stumbling across was littered and toxic, yet, he was standing and taking a step. His eyes were as big as Mexican gold pieces and his mouth opened with joy. -And there was his Dad. The young Father was so excited that he began to applaud and when he did, everyone in the line began to follow suit.

When I saw this, it was as if heaven invaded earth. It literally changed my life and gave me a perspective of the Father's love towards me that ....well, more than 15 years later, I'm writing a book on it.

I see you and I in the wide eyed look of that precious little boy. Yes we are a mess and we are living in a mess but Papa loves for us to get up anyway and move /forward.

A BLESSED MESS

The bible tells a story just like this in John chapter 4. Jesus was traveling from Jerusalem in the south, to Galilee in the north and taking the quickest route, He went through Samaria. Tired and thirsty, our Lord sat by Jacob's Well and sent his disciples about a half mile away, to buy some food. It was the hottest part of the day when a Samaritan woman came to the well to draw water.

The relationship between the Jews and the Samaritans was mess. The difference of cultural views on how and where to worship were a mess. In fact, everything relational in this woman's life was a mess. She had been married five times and the guy she was living with now, wasn't her husband. I think she had wondered what the point would be after so many failed marriages.

This woman was a mess and in order for him to reach her, Jesus had to be willing to get involved in a mess. His typically amazing heart took over and He got as messy as was required, without complaint.

In His encounter with the woman at the well, Jesus broke three major Jewish customs: first, he spoke to a woman; second, she was a Samaritan woman, a group the Jews despised; and third, he asked her to get him a drink of water, which would have made him ceremonially unclean from using her cup or jar.

It was a mess and Jesus dived in head first to help this lady get a cup of *"living water."* He was so anxious for her to come out of the darkness she was living in, he threw his own culture and traditions out the window to reach her.

She was shocked, then the disciples showed up with a bucket from KFC and they were also shocked.

Leaving behind her water jar, the woman returned to town, inviting the people to *"Come, see a man who told me all that I ever did."* (John 4:29)

Excited by what the woman told them, the Samaritans came out and begged Jesus to stay with them. So Jesus stayed two more days, teaching the Samaritan people all about the Kingdom.

When he left, the people told the woman, *"... we have heard for ourselves, and we know that this is indeed the Savior of the world."* John 4:42

Jesus was literally born to bless a mess. From the miracle in the midst of struggle at Bethlehem to the miracle of salvation at the struggle of the cross. I am here to tell you that Jesus is not intimidated by messy environments and ugly situations.

He breaks out into applause the moment any of us get up and stumble /forward. He jumps down into the trash and says "Come to Papa!"

THE FIGHT FOR GREATNESS
So did the disciples walk around as stereotypes of words like powerless, ineffective, ineffectual, inadequate, weak, feeble, useless, worthless? No! People who remain close to Jesus take on bold new identities.

These magnificent misfits, although a motley crew, actually argued over issues of greatness in spite of their mess. They were not afraid they would get into trouble for messing up. So they went /forward and the rest of us are blessed for it.

GOD THOUGHTS AND MEDITATIONS

People who encounter Jesus are encouraged by the Holy Spirit to move /forward from where they are at. List some of the places where God is telling you must move /forward from here.

_____

_____

_____

_____

What motivation do you have for moving /forward. What will be the joyous result of moving from where you are? What could be the consequences of not fighting for /forward?

_____

_____

_____

_____

Are those consequences acceptable to you? Are they acceptable to God? Ask Him and see what He tells you. _____

_____

_____

_____

What are some mistakes you fear and some failures you fear that keep you from moving /forward?
Can you still be in right standing with God, blessed and highly favored, even if you did not succeed in every way? The answer to that is a great big Yes!!!_____

_____

_____

_____

When the disciples hung out with Jesus they began to argue over who was the greatest among them. How is the Lord inviting you into better relationship with Him? Since He has never suffered from identity issues He knows His greatness. Can you just stop and worship Him for how great He really is to you?

Quote from this Chapter
"Religion trains people to think the worst thing that can happen is to do something wrong. What Jesus teaches is the worst thing that can happen is for you to do nothing at all!"

"God takes advancement and multiplication very seriously. In this parable (Matthew 25) His wrath is displayed, not at the mistakes we make in moving /forward, but in the mistake of refusing to move at all."

Points to Ponder:
(1) We cannot let messed up things keep us from fighting for /forward. When we do not move, we are paralyzed and the record shows Jesus loves to heal people who are paralyzed.

(2) According to the gospel of account of Jesus' encounter with the woman at the well, God is not ashamed or scared in any way of our mess. He is totally willing to get involved right where we are to help move us /forward. In the Kingdom, the cleanup comes after the progress /forward and the encounter with God happens in the mess, not just after the mess is cleaned up.

(3) People who are convinced they are messed up are always going to mess up.

(4) People who are convinced they can't mess up, can't mess up.

(5) In the Kingdom, Identity, or who we believe we are in Christ, is everything to unlocking supernatural power and upgrade.

_____
_____
_____
_____
_____
_____
_____
_____

Here's a place for you to write down thoughts, scriptures, notes...
We just went through a lot and you might need to sort through it.

_____
_____
_____
_____
_____
_____
_____
_____
_____
_____
_____
_____
_____
_____

CHAPTER TWO
The Fight For What Can Be

So we are learning that we must trust in the heart of God and in the power of His grace. We are discovering that He is not prepared to punish us for mistakes in moving /forward. He is prepared to pick us up. God is passionate about our progression. He has a much higher value on your personal growth than He does for your punishment.

> *I will heal their faithlessness; I will love them freely,*
> *for My anger is turned away from [Israel].*
> Hosea 14: 4

Since He made you to be warrior, He knows that if you don't fight for /forward, you will fight for what does not matter. He says to you the same thing He said to Joshua three different times when He commanded him to move /forward into the promise land.

"FEAR NOT"

When we are afraid to move from where we are, we will settle for something that once was, rather than what could be. That's what this chapter is about. The fight for what once was, is a fight for what is irrelevant and insignificant. It's the wrong fight to be in.

ENTER THE DRAGON : RELIGION
Whatever used to be a long time ago, religion likes to call that "godliness." We must resist the Amish like temptation to canonize an era if we are going to tap into how God is moving today.

When you keep your head stuck in the sands of the past, you will never move /forward.

AN EYE FOR GREAT THINGS
An alternative to glorifying an era and a proper view of the past is to see how Great God is in the past. When you look for Jesus in your past you learn to see Him in your present.

The angles that circle the throne are a special breed of tripped out creative magnificence. They don't look anything like the little fat Caucasian babies with wings they are so often portrayed. They look like something from the Sci-fi channel.

Revelation 4:6 *Before the throne there was[e] a sea of glass, like crystal. And in the midst of the throne, and around the throne, were four living creatures full of eyes in front and in back. 7 The first living creature was like a lion, the second living creature like a calf, the third living creature had a face like a man, and the fourth living creature was like a flying eagle. 8 The four living creatures, each having six wings, were full of eyes around and within. And they do not rest day or night, saying:"Holy, holy, holy, Lord God Almighty, Who was and is and is to come!"*

It's strange enough that each one has four sides and four separate faces but have you noticed the word says that their bodies are covered in "eyes"?

They literally see God in the past, present and future all at the same time and every time they circle the throne they see how Great God has been, how great God is now and how great God is going to be in the future.

"Holy Holy Holy is the Lord God Almighty who was, who is and who is yet to come!"

I want to be like that. I don't just want to see my past I want to see how great God has been in my past. Once I see that, I want to see how great God is now in every part of my life and from there I want to see how great God is, /forward from here.

KEEP YOUR EYE ON THE GOD BALL

To be too fixated on the past for the sake of the past can be toxic. When this happens, our fight for greatness gets replaced with a fight for preserving history and that is where it really gets ugly.

You can see how ugly it gets in the hateful and even murderous acts of the sixties civil rights movement.

The fight for what once was, totally wrecked the music industry at the turn of the last century as they refused to embrace what was digital for what used to be vinyl.

We could go on and on but in the body of Christ we see churches closing down and loosing influence over culture and the marketplace. We even see Christian nations losing nearly all ground over the fight for what once was, instead of having the passion to fight for what can be. An unhealthy fascination of the past is toxic to moving /forward.

A TROLL UNDER THE BRIDGE

In the late eighties, I spent a lot of time under the I-45 bridge in downtown Dallas. The huge gathering spot of homeless and indigent there was called *Shanty Town* by the big city press.

I sang and played guitar for a Christian rock band called *Destiny*. We rocked the area and handed out thousands of pounds of food to people without jobs, without hope and some who hadn't had teeth or even minds in years.

It was a real wild west show and right up my adventure loving alley, back then. It was always fun, powerful, and always unpredictable. Jesus loves to bless the rejected and the messed up.

So I was not surprised when several messed up people unplugged my P.A. system in mid song and actually proceeded to push over the 8 foot tall wooden cross we had stood up out there.

However, I was surprised, to see these messed up people were not homeless but were actually from the church just several blocks away.

As a pastor for nearly 20 years, I want to say again, this is not about bashing church or any one denomination. The problem is not just church, the problem with church is when we partner with a spirit that isn't the Holy Spirit.

CHRISTIANS NEED JESUS
Sometimes it's just real that "Christians" need to be saved. A team of chosen frozen had come to preserve the history of God's move from years ago. One which included the pulpit of their congregation in days gone by. This move of God, which we were a part of, was not on their outdated spiritual radar. So they didn't recognize it as God and felt like they were doing God a service in wiping us out.

"We're Methodists and we don't do this." said an ugly man in a good looking suit. "This is America and we don't need missionaries. We also don't need you encouraging people to stay and feeding people who are not welcome in this part of town.

A RUDE DUDE IN A CRUDE MOOD
I wish I could tell you that The Spirit of the Lord rose up within me and I prophetically announced a word of righteousness that rent the heavens. I was young and green saved. So true to form, I informed him that though he was Methodist, I was Texan and

commenced to teach him and another fellow what the business end of a stick can do in the hands of a properly motivated 19 year old, bull rider from Johnson County.

The police arrived and had I not left in a bigger hurry that allowed me to get my equipment, I would have gone to jail. I lost my P.A system that day and my giant cross. I barely escaped with my guitar and my testimony. Again, I was young.

Like Woodrow Call from Lonesome Dove, I could not abide by his rude behavior. Now nearly twenty five years later, I look at that day and see a young man full of passion in big need of the fruit of self-control. I also see a group of people who had given away their fight for greatness, for a fight to preserve insignificance. My anger has since turned to Pity.

MOVERS AND SHAKERS
I heard Graham Cooke say the greatest threat to a new move of God is what you think about the last move of God. It's not about the method of how God moves, it's about God moving and we must be willing to follow Him /forward.

Just because we recognize God did something great at a certain time in a certain way, doesn't mean we have to canonize the era and method.

Look at all the different ways Jesus reached the people He came into contact with. From turning water into wine to clipping the ear of Malchus, back to his head. From preaching to the crowds to visiting Zacheus at his house, Jesus never used a single method to bring people into the Kingdom.

All of them were the right method but none of them were the only method. As His resurrection would prove, you can't keep Jesus nailed down or in a box.

In an exclusive interview with Nicodemus, Jesus warned of the in-exclusiveness of method in the creative ways He touches the heart of men.

The wind blows where ever it pleases. You hear its sound but you cannot tell where it comes from or where it is going, so it is with everyone born for the Spirit. John 3:8 NIV

DESTINY VS HISTORY
It just so happens, at the time I am writing this chapter, I am facing south on a northbound train. The lounge car on AMTRAK allows you to sit at a table and Steve Jobs allowed me to type out a book while heading back home from a trip.

From my seat, I can see where I have been but not where I am going. All of the scenery around me moves from my sides into what is behind me and that's all I can perceive.

So much of the church sits just like this. Fixated on history and oblivious to destiny but that church train will never move any of us /forward.

The goodness of God is not just seen in the past but is calling from the future. People who fight for what can be, understand that God says their Destiny is much greater than their history.

From a seated backward perspective, everything in the future is scary to the religious. Instead of teaching the book of revelation as a study on the majesty of Christ, they use it to warn us to not have social security numbers.

Fear of the future and a fixed fascination of the past are the enemies of upgrade.

It was the same way in Jesus' day. He turned to the religious and called it like Babe Ruth, hitting a home run out of the ball park.

You search the Scriptures, for in them you think you have eternal life; and these are they which testify of Me. But you are not willing to come to Me that you may have life.
John 5:38-39

In other words, Jesus said, you're willing to know the scriptures or the things written long ago, but you are not willing to know me. You search the scriptures but won't come, or move /forward to me.

You have settled for history and given up experience. You have settled for revelation without accepting the invitation to personally encounter who the scriptures were talking about. You won't move /forward!

They didn't recognize Him because He wasn't in the same place and working in the same method, He had in days before. They would not go /forward and it cost them everything.

But that's not you. Your Destiny is much greater than your History and you're not afraid to fight for it.

You have a great respect for the scripture but a higher value for personally knowing the author of the scriptures.

You have turned your chair from looking at what is behind the train to what is in front of it.

Sometimes you smell it before you see it and you might even be willing to take a bite before you even know what it is. That's the trust part again and fear is long gone when trust rules and reigns.

Your fight is not for what used to be, but serves as a footing for you to boldly leap /forward into the promise of what God is telling you can be.

You know what He has for you is not in your past. So go ahead, take a bite and move /forward.

Oh, taste and see that the LORD is good;
Blessed is the man who trusts in Him! Psalms 34:8

GOD THOUGHTS AND MEDITATIONS
THE FIGHT FOR WHAT CAN BE

People who encounter Jesus are encouraged to consider more than what once was. The Holy Spirit will convict us of wasted energy on things that really don't matter. Can you list any places where you tend to fight for what once was, more than what really can be? List some areas where it is easy for you to be distracted.

_____

_____

_____

_____

The Holy Spirit causes us to dream way past what once was. Can you articulate what can be in some areas of your life?

_____

_____

_____

_____

_____

_____

A proper view of the reality of God in your past will enable you to see him in your Future. It's the job of the Holy Spirit to show us Jesus. Ask Him to show you where Jesus was in the difficult parts of your life and List How He helped you and sustained you. _____

_____

_____

_____

_____

Quote from this Chapter

"Whatever used to be a long time ago, religion likes to call that "godliness." We must resist the Amish like temptation to canonize an era if we are going to tap into how God is moving today."

"An alternative to glorifying an era and a proper view of the past is to see how Great God is in the past. When you look for Jesus in your past you learn to see Him in your present."

Points to Ponder:

(1) We are learning to confront the fearful parts of our heart that does not want to move from what is familiar to us. The fight for what can be should replace the fight to preserve the traditions and methods of the past. We cannot move /forward until this part of or life is confronted

(2) *The wind blows where ever it pleases. You hear its sound but you cannot tell where it comes from or where it is going, so it is with everyone born for the Spirit.* John 3:8 NIV

We cannot nail down the Holy Spirit to any one particular method. God reserves the right to unlimited and unrestricted expression of His heart.

He loves to surprise us in how he shows up and where He shows up. We should recognize him by His Heart, His Spirit and by His Fruit more than looking for a method of how God moves.

If we insist on a particular method, we spend all of our energy on fighting for a way God once moved rather than fighting for dream of the heart of God.

PERSONAL THOUGHTS AND VICTORIES

_____

_____

_____

_____

_____

_____

_____

_____

_____

_____

_____

_____

_____

_____

_____

_____

_____

_____

_____

_____

_____

_____

_____

_____

_____

"The goodness of God is not just seen in the past but is calling from the future. People who fight for what can be, understand that God says their Destiny is much greater than their history."
Troy Brewer : Living Life /Forward

CHAPTER THREE
The Fight for His Heart

Robert the Bruce remains one of Scotland's great national heroes right up there with William Wallace. Now if you don't know who Wallace or the Bruce are, I bet you know who Mel Gibson is.

Mel Gibson is the actor who has played everything from *The Road Warrior* to the hands of Jesus in his famous Easter movie, but the movie I think he is most famous for is his Brit-bashing *Braveheart.*

Gibson plays Wallace but the title Braveheart is actually about Robert the Bruce.

"I have nothing," Robert says "Men fight for me because if they do not, I throw them off my land and I starve their wives and their children. Those men who bled the ground red at Falkirk, they fought for William Wallace, and he fights for something that I never had. And I took it from him, when I betrayed him. I saw it in his face on the battlefield and it's tearing me apart."

His old father replies, "All men betray. All lose heart."

"I don't wanna lose heart. I wanna believe as he does."

I remember sitting in the theatre and hearing those lines for the first time. I felt the failure of the character on screen and like him, I wanted to believe the way another believes. It was 1995 and I was about to launch OpenDoor Church from the ground up with only seven people to gather for our first service. I needed courage. I wanted to see my life the way The King, I'm not talking about Elvis, sees my life. Yes Jesus invades my movie watching and I tend to fully love it when He does.

KINGS CROSS
Several years later on a missions trip to England, I spent a day on a train from London to Edinburg. Leanna and I stepped out of the station and saw the incredible Castle for the first time. It took my breath away!

We saw the royal mile, a kilt shop and the house of John Knox. But it was at the actual Castle I first heard the following story. The hero of Scottish independence didn't betray William Wallace but was inspired by him.

To the strains of Border bagpipes and medieval poetry in praise of freedom, Robert the Bruce, the warrior King, lay on his deathbed about to die.

Long exhausted from a life of having to battle not just the English, but Scotland's own nobility, its church, its monasteries, the Pope and the national spirit of defeatism itself. He was a very old man at the age of only 54. It was June 7, 1329.

So the Bruce found himself lying on his death bed with minutes before he finally met his maker. Around him were friends, family and his great right-hand-man, Sir James Douglas. Hero of the Scottish wars of independence and bogey man to the British of the day.

The King's mind still alive within a body some believe was dying of leprosy, he called Sir James over to his bedside.

Barely able to speak, in a hushed voice the king told Sir James what he wanted.

"Douglas, help me." he whispered, "When I die you must cut my heart from my body and take it on a crusade. Bury my heart in the Holy sepulcher in Jerusalem."

Moments later, the king passed into eternity and the loyal knight plunged his dagger into the king's chest. As others gasped, he sawed open the rib cage and removed the king's heart. Marching from the room and covered in blood, he found a blacksmith and made a lead casket which he then hung on a chain around his neck. Douglas formed a volunteer Scottish army later that year and set off on the crusade he had promised.

Off they went, but when they arrived in Spain, Douglas discovered that it was crawling with Saracens and Moors. Vastly outnumbered, perhaps even by as many as five to one, the Saracens had fought off the initial charge and began a counter charge at the Battle of Teba.

Sir James and some fellow knights found themselves isolated from the main force. They were about to be surrounded and he knew that they would soon be dragged from their mounts and killed. Because they were leaders, their death would be likely to be long and horrible.

As Sir James was about to be overwhelmed, he took the heart, held it by the chain, swung it around his head like a hammer at the Olympic Games and flung it into the fray. Charging in after it and screaming at the top of his voice, "Lead on Braveheart, as thou dost! Forward, Forward!"

As the heart fell to the ground, Douglas leapt on top of it, protecting his king to the last while commanding his fellow knights.

"Fight for the heart of your King!"

What greater love can a man have for his king? And that is where the name "Braveheart" originated. A dead Robert the Bruce, not a live William Wallace but none the less an amazing true story.

It is also the reason why the motto of the Scottish clan Douglas remains "/Forward" to this day.

THE FIGHT FOR HIS HEART

The passionate heart of our King will never be satisfied with anything mediocre. That's why He is dealing with you on so many different things at once. When you fight for the heart of the King you fight for greatness within your own life.

Jesus did not live and die on this earth for you and I to live defeated, insignificant lives. He would love us and treat us like kings if that was all that we did but it is not what He came to do.

It turns out, there is a big fight, instead of a vacation, for the heart of the King in your life. I want to encourage you to become who He has called you to be.

> *For many are called, but few are chosen*
> John 22:14

The masses are invited but there are very few actually honored. Not many accept the call of this Brave heart to move /forward into our fullest potential.

The heart of this King is a supernatural heart which says *Permission granted.* If we accept this calling and move /forward, submitting our lives and conforming our lives to the image of his plan, we find ourselves no longer in shameful places.

Instead of their shame my people will receive a double portion, and instead of disgrace they will rejoice in their inheritance;

and so they will inherit a double portion in their land,
and everlasting joy will be theirs.
Isaiah 61:7

SOUL FOOD AND SPIRIT FOOD

People who live with their head on the chest of the Lord, in Rhythm with the heart of God, like John at the last supper, are people with great revelation.

Revelation doesn't just say, "It's out there." Revelation says "Go get it!" A revelation of the word of God is not supposed to be the end game of our walk. It is merely the beginning.

The Spirit of the Lord breathes upon the scriptures, or upon whatever it is you are looking at, and suddenly you perceive supernatural revelation.

That's great but that's not what it is for. God doesn't care if you know about Him, He wants us to know him by personal experience.

Revelation is not given to add another wrinkle to our brain. Revelation is an invitation to step /forward into experience with God.

Understanding the purpose of revelation is the power behind it. Revelation is a key to unlocking barriers so you can move /forward into what God says CAN be.

It's an invitation to fight for His heart.

AN ACQUIRED TASTE

The scripture doesn't say, oh smell and see that the Lord is good. The smell is supposed to be a mouth- watering invitation to take a big bite. Just like that, revelation is a green light to experience

God in the way He is being reveled to you. You have to be willing to go /forward and moving /forward into experience, requires trust.

Oh, taste and see that the LORD is good;
Blessed is the man who trusts in Him! Psalms 34:8

Tasting is all about personal experience and trusting is all about believing you will not get into trouble.
We have already covered some of this.

We must be willing to smell the savor of things not yet experienced in Christ, instead of holding our nose for the parts of God that are much more common.

When we forget we are supposed to look /forward, we settle for what others have experienced, trusting their taste buds instead of the Lord. When we are not savoring what can be, we settle for the documented pallet of the past.

I wonder who the first guy was who decided to eat an egg or even a raw oyster? That's courage. Just like that, a woman crawled on her knees to touch the hem of the garment of Jesus without any historical reference to go by. That also is courage and I would say, desperation motivated both of them. Because of her courage to go /forward, she experienced God in a way like nobody else ever had.

She got her supernatural upgrade and it saved her life. Good thing she didn't listen to the skeptics and the religious of her day. She would have missed it.

This was a woman of faith. Real faith. When we don't find life in new ways, we settle for what is written about God. That's a really safe kind of Pseudo-faith. It requires little to none, personal experience and encounter. It assumes no responsibility for knowing God's heart today.

We become bible thumpers instead of Heart listeners. We learn the culture of our denominations instead of the ways of God.

That's not you. Fight through the fear of the unknown and fight for the heart of your King. The next level is just past your next victory in this fight.

GOD THOUGHTS AND MEDITATIONS FOR THE FIGHT FOR HIS HEART

What are some things that you personally think about the amazing heart of Jesus? How is His heart like a Father and a friend towards you? List some of those amazing qualities.

_____
_____
_____
_____
_____
_____
_____

What are some areas of your own heart that need to be conformed to His heart? Let the Holy Spirit take you to some key areas in your life and let Him show you what His heart is towards those people and towards that situation. List your thoughts.

_____
_____
_____
_____
_____
_____
_____

Quote from this Chapter
"The passionate heart of our King will never be satisfied with anything mediocre. That's why He is dealing with you on so many different things at once. When you fight for the heart of the King you fight for greatness within your own life."

"The heart of this King is a supernatural heart which says *Permission granted.* If we accept this calling and move /forward, submitting our lives and conforming our lives to the image of his plan, we find ourselves no longer in shameful places."

Points to Ponder:

(1) God's heart is that of a passionate, poet/warrior, like King David's heart. He never settles for mediocre when He can go after that which is amazing.

(2) Any revelation we receive from God is not supposed to make us smarter. Revelation is supposed to be an invitation to personally experience Him in the way He is revealing Himself to us. It is always about knowing Him in a greater way as opposed to knowing about Him in a greater way.

(3) When I fight for His heart, I fight for what God is passionate about. This means when I fight to do what He has called me to do, I must fight to do it in a way that displays His amazing heart. What good is it to feed the poor if I don't demonstrate the heart of God in how I feed the poor? What good is it to have a church service and preach the gospel if I don't treat people right and honor those I am preaching to? Fighting for the heart of the King means fighting to display how good God is in what He thinks is important.

_____

_____

_____

_____

_____

_____

_____

_____

"The passionate heart of our King will never be satisfied with anything mediocre. That's why He is dealing with you on so many different things at once. When you fight for the heart of the King you fight for greatness within your own life."
Troy Brewer : Living Life /Forward

CHAPTER FOUR
The Fight for momentum

One Victory causes another victory to happen. That's why victory must become a lifestyle.

PLAY IT AGAIN SAM
Central America is an amazing place. I especially love Costa Rica and Guatemala. You see such amazing things that you never see in the states.
Volcanos, waterfalls and coffee plantations are big on my list of ewws and ahhs. I'm like a kid on the 4th of July on every mission trip to go to the other Americas.

About a decade ago, I saw something at the airport that taught me a lesson on /Forward.

I witnessed a crashed Cuban airliner that went off the edge of the runway in Guatemala City, Guatemala. It was big. I think it was a 747. The wreckage is still there and I expect it will be for years because I noticed families had taken up residence in it.

When I got back to the states, I did some research on the airport in an attempt to find out what had happened. From various reports, it seems the fatal crash is a simple story of momentum. The pilot had never landed on the short runway before and he landed much later than he should have.

At the end of the runway is a cliff that drops off into the slums below. That poor pilot desperately tried to stop his aircraft as he slammed on the brakes and reversed his thrusters, but because of the momentum of that huge jet airliner, he ran out of runway and went over the cliff.

At the end of that same runway, as we were taking off, I could see grooves in the pavement that went straight off into nothing. Awesome is the power of momentum.

It is important, as teachable people, to be selective and intentional on how things impact us. I didn't want to forget about this because I knew God had a word for me in it.

Brother Webster defines momentum like this

WEBSTER DICTIONARY:

(1) The quantity of motion in a moving body,
being always proportioned to the quantity
of matter multiplied into the velocity; impetus.

(2) An impelling force of strength.

There is an impelling force of strength involved in the act of moving /forward. Never underestimate the power of momentum.

God has designed things so that when one thing moves towards another there becomes an amplified strength in proportion to the rate it is moving.

In other words, progressive people get more progressive. Learning people get more power to learn. Giving people get more power to give; loving people get more power to love.

Jesus puts it this way.

Whoever has will be given more, and he will have an
abundance. Whoever does not have,
even what he has will be taken from him.
Matthew 13:12

The power to upgrade and go from the cheap seats to the box seats in any area of our life is in direct proportion to our willingness to move /forward within that arena.

The key is that when God grants us a breakthrough we must be prepared to go to the next level again and again and again without stopping.

The Kingdom is not for people who fear change and pine for the good old days. The Kingdom is transformational and so are the people who go through it with an impelling force of strength.

And from the days of John the Baptist until now the kingdom of heaven suffers violence, and the violent take it by force.
Matthew 11:12

If you're not sure what Jesus was saying in this text, maybe this newer translation will help you sink your teeth into it.

From the days of John the Baptist until now, the kingdom of heaven has been forcefully advancing,
and forceful men lay hold of it.
Matthew 11:12 NIV

FROM HERE TO ETERNITY
In the Kingdom we do not fight for victory but we fight *FROM* victory.

From Victory to Victory in a momentum of God's goodness. Scripture explains it in different ways in several different books. Here are some examples.

Here a little there a little. Line upon line. Precept upon precept.
Isaiah 28:13

You learn the next supernatural principle from the force of strength from the last principle you learned. Learners learn more and gain momentum in learning.

From faith to faith
Romans 1:17

You leap to the next level of faith from the victory of your current breakthrough in faith. When God heals you of a cold, it is from that place you begin to reach for faith in healing for a disease. When you see someone healed of a disease, it is from that place you reach for faith to raise the dead. This momentum comes from encounter and personal experience only.

From glory to glory
2 Corinthians 3:18

Glory is when our right relationship with God becomes manifest. Moses so wanted to see the glory of God and he wanted to see Him face to face. We move into deeper and deeper places of relationship from deep places of relationship.

That's why the bibles says in Psalms 42:7 *"Deep calls unto deep..."*

Skill is developed from practice and God take us into what is extraordinary and makes it a common way of life.

From everlasting unto everlasting
Psalms 41:13

Eternity invades the temporary and heaven invades earth through the momentum of the last way eternity moved into time. Not necessarily the same way but from the momentum of it.

Think about how much effort the enemy puts into breaking your momentum. Instead of an unstoppable moving freight train, he tries to keep you moving like a squirrel where you take a step and freeze up for a while.

This principle and promise of momentum excites me and motivates me. It says once I start moving God honors me and gives me grace to move all the more.

THE GAME CHANGER
Jehovah Nissi is one of the 16 God names listed in the old testament. You probably have heard of Jehovah Jireh, The Lord our provider or Jehovah Rapha, the Lord our Healer.

If you have walked with God for very long, you have probably met Jehovah Sneaky, though He's not listed in the bible, I have met this part of God many times. That's the part of Jesus that doesn't tell you everything you are signing up for.

Jehovah Nissi is a legitimate name in the bible and one you need to learn to call upon on. Jehovah Nissi is the game changing side of the Lord. The momentum changer.

The Lord is our Banner or Jehovah Nissi speaks of a battlefield where suddenly everything changes because the kings banner is now in the fray. It means the King himself is fighting the fight.

Everything changes when you can see Jesus on your battlefield. It is from that momentum that you pick up your sword, get off of the ground and scream in the face of the enemy again.

THE BOTTOM LINE
When it all comes down to it, the violent part of moving /forward in the Kingdom is to be taken head on and never from our flanks or from behind.

The armor is for Living Life /Forward.

The armor that God equips us with in Ephesians Chapter six covers everything but our butt. It is not for people who turn their backs to see what is behind them. It is for people positioned to move /forward.

You and I are not meant to be Lott's wife but the bride of Christ. A warrior bride and supernatural juggernaut that can't be stopped, denied or ignored.

GOD THOUGHTS AND MEDITATIONS

_____

_____

_____

_____

_____

_____

_____

_____

_____

_____

_____

_____

_____

_____

_____

_____

_____

_____

_____

_____

_____

_____

_____

From everlasting unto everlasting
Psalms 41:13

"Eternity invades the temporary and heaven invades earth through the momentum of the last way eternity moved into time. Not necessarily the same way but from the momentum of it."
Troy Brewer : Living Life /Forward

SECTION TWO:
AN UNDISCOVERED COUNTRY

Sam: "This is it."
Frodo: "This is what?"
"If I take one more step, I'll be the farthest away from home I have ever been."
— *The lord of the rings.*

"Where am I go'in I dont know. When will I There, I aint certain. All that I know is I am on my way." — *Paint your wagon*

Now the LORD had said to Abram, Get you out of your country, and from your kindred, and from your father's house, to a land that I will show you:
— *The Bible, Genesis 12:1*

"Life is a series of adjustments; You can make changes along the way, but if you don't start moving /forward you'll never get anywhere!"
— *Kimora Lee Simmons*

CHAPTER FIVE
Off The Map

In section Two I want us to move from the fight to move /Forward to the actual process of discovery. There is a whole different paradigm we discover when we win the battle, move /forward and actually stomp around in these new and better places. There is an immediate problem with the new level in that we are unfamiliar with it. I call those places off the map.

...and lo, I am with you always, even unto the end of the world.
Matthew 28:20

The place where Jesus promises to meet us is not on anybody's map. It's off the chart, past the end of what you know as your world. It's that place He is constantly inviting us into. Let's unpack this.

THE GREAT DIVIDE
History records that when Alexander the great came to the Indian Ocean, he wept because to him, there was no more world to conquer.

He had no idea of the Chinese empire or the Japanese shogun warriors. He never could have imagined the Mayan city of Cerros with its complex of temples and ball courts in Meso-America. Nor could he have envisioned the already fierce Zulu nation in South Africa. I wonder how he would have dealt with the Venicones of modern day Scotland? A group that later, even the Romans couldn't take out.

There was actually much more for Alexander to conquer but he was completely limited to a map.

You and I are called to be greater than Alexander ever could be, because we have no such limitations.

See, I am doing a new thing! Now it springs up; do you not perceive it? I am making a way in the wilderness and streams in the wasteland
Isaiah 43:19

The wildness is the wilderness because it isn't inhabited. It's in those uncharted places He makes a way or a path of progression for each of us.

He causes it to "spring up." In other words you don't know it's there until you go there. It is hidden until you get there. It jumps up like a Jack-in-the-box which is triggered by your arrival.

Because of this part of God's heart, He will ask you to try new things without any explanation what so ever.

He will tell you to do something that you have never done before and He will ask you to try things you don't have any map or grid for whatsoever.

This is God moving you /forward.

He doesn't care if you are a professional speaker when he calls you to speak to great people. - Just ask Moses.

He doesn't care if people like you when He calls you to have influence as a prophet. Just ask Jeremiah.

He doesn't care what everybody thinks worship should look like when He tells you to let it all hang out for his heart. Just ask David.

He doesn't care if everything in your culture tells you to do something exactly opposite. Just ask Peter when God told him to eat *unclean* food.

The best part of God is not found in the outer court of the temple where everything is familiar, but rather in the holy of holies where most people never see.

He wants us to discover what others have never seen and we need look no further than within our own lives.

> *Neither shall they say, See here! or, see there! for, behold,*
> *the kingdom of God is within you*
> Luke 17:21

HIS HEART IN THE HEADLINES
On any given day, I tend to pound keys, play guitar and tell tall tales. Though I am a lifelong resident of Johnson County, Texas, I am also a world traveler who has the privilege of being in front of many different kinds of faces.

As the world becomes aware that we are actually a global people, for me, I am thinking it's more about a corporate body. Because of that, I think God can speak to you and me from events and circumstances that are not even within our region. Yes, I'm weird like that.

See if this doesn't tilt your Jesus pinball machine.

IF IT HAD BEEN A SNAKE...
In 2005, authorities released news of a newly discovered giant waterfall hidden away, less than 15 miles from a park headquarters. A 400 foot tall cascading wonder had been there all the time in Shasta County, and nobody knew it.

Four hundred feet of raging whitewater sounds hard to miss. But that's what happened in California and I believe it was a prophetic voice for you and I.

Something so magnificent waiting to be discovered could only be seen from above. It was found through satellite images.

Sometimes you can't see the forest for the trees and sometimes you can't see the 400 foot waterfall because it is off the trail everybody traditionally walks on. This waterfall was there all the time but it wasn't on the map.

I hear the heart-beat of the Father in that event. I thought, "God knew it was there the whole time and He specifically waited for a 15 year park employee to find it for the rest of us." What a great day for the Lord that must have been.

In 1990, when NASA deployed the Hubble telescope through the space shuttle Discovery, they were determined to see what had never been seen before.

I think God gets excited anytime anybody does that.

LOOKING SKYWARD
At one point, they aimed toward a very dark, seemingly empty part of space and waited ten days for the images to come back. Not only did they discover that there were hidden stars, where it seemed there were none, but millions, even billions in that one "empty" place. They counted over 1500 Galaxies, with each containing millions of stars, in one tiny area about the size of a dime at 75 yards away.

How patient God is for us to finally discover what He has always had there for us! I don't know about you, but I'm not like that.

It is amazing to me that He is so anxious for us to see it and so patient with our inability to find it. He's just awesome.

The sombrero Galaxy was there for a long time before anybody ever looked at it and said, "Wow!" The entire North American continent and western world sat silent for a long long time before Europe ever knew or heard of it. El Capitan and Yosemite Valley stood rock solid in pristine condition for eons before the Paiute Indians made their first camp fire or the great John Muir ever stomped around there.

It took adventurist people, who would not be confined to what was known, to unlock it for the rest of us. And so it is with the things of God.

"This is God's Message, the God who made earth, made it livable and lasting, known everywhere as God: 'Call to me and I will answer you. I'll tell you marvelous and wondrous things that you could never figure out on your own.
Jeremiah 33:3 from The Message Bible

THE TALKING HEADS

There is an arrogant, cerebral bunch among us who actually believe God is confined to their understanding of the scripture. I appreciate the fact they have ten pound heads but it's really not very attractive.

Not only is God not limited to our understanding of the scripture but He is not limited to scripture at all.

Even the scripture says Jesus does all kinds of things that is not even recorded in the bible. The very last verse of arguably the greatest Gospel, John, says this,

*And there are also many other things that Jesus did, which if
they were written one by one, I suppose that even the world
itself could not contain the books that would be written. Amen*
John 21:25

The bible says you could fill up the world with books that were
written to record the works of Jesus that are not recorded in the
bible!

In other words, God reserves the right to do tons of things not
written down or mapped out.

The Bible declares that there are some things God speaks which
He doesn't allow to be written but they are for the hearer only.

*And when the seven thunders had sounded, I was about to write,
but I heard a voice from heaven saying, "Seal up what the seven
thunders have said, and do not write it down."*
Revelation 10:4

I would never advocate any form of departure from the bible, so
if I am pegging your cringe meter, dial it down. I'm saying that
you have permission to experience God in a powerful way that
is way beyond our limited understanding of scripture.

When the woman crawled to touch the hem of His garment to be
healed she was doing that not because she had a scripture to act
on, but a revelation of His heart towards her.

When those knuckle heads tore apart the roof and lowered down
their friend into the house where Jesus was teaching, they were
not acting within the confines of what was written. This was off
the chart!

They discovered a part of God's heart that no one else had before.

It is for this reason, Paul calls the gift of God (Jesus) *indescribable*.

Thanks be to God for his indescribable gift!
2 Corinthians 9:12

The gift of Jesus is not indescribable because there are no words, He is indescribable because there are not enough words to describe the endless way He is moving and being.

So you think the Lord is calling you to go to school, adopt a baby, start a business or pray for a miracle?

Do not discount it because it is nothing you are familiar with. Being familiar with His voice and knowing His heart is the premier catalyst for finding highways that spring up in uninhabited places.

When the map runs out, move /forward and chart it out for the rest of us.

_____

_____

_____

_____

_____

_____

_____

See, I am doing a new thing! Now it springs up; do you not perceive it? I am making a way in the wilderness and streams in the wasteland. Isaiah 43:19

"The wildness is the wilderness because it isn't inhabited. It's in those uncharted places He makes a way or a path of progression for each of us."
Troy Brewer : Living Life /Forward

CHAPTER SIX

Third Stage

There is an amazing pattern throughout the scriptures of our journey of progression that I can't wait to show you.

I first discovered this pattern through the teachings of Howard Richardson at a tent revival in 1986. I was only 19 years old in August of that year and had only been born again in May.

It was super-hot that summer and there I sat at an old school-Pentecostal, tent revival. The long haired preacher ranted his revelation with the back drop of an organ playing through the entire three hours of teaching and prophesying. He came complete with a white suit and a fancy watch.

Just as I was about to wonder about this guy, he began teaching and the power of God rocked my world. The Lord taught me real quick that I didn't know squat and 25 years later I am still blown away at the anointing and the revelation of that man.

At the end of the first night He made his way to the very back row where I had parked myself in case I needed to bolt. He spoke in a booming voice but with a gentle spirit and said, "God showed me you're involved in a court case."

I did have a court date looming on the horizon and he had my full attention. He went on to say that he would give me a word but that I had to come every night of the week and just sit in the presence of God because God was going to change me. He said that if I did that, He believed the Lord would give me something prophetic on Friday night that would totally change my life.

It's a good thing I was young because I probably wouldn't jump through that hoop for anybody today. It was a tall order for me to get off of work, drive over an hour to where this was at and stay past 11 every evening. But, I did and think God I did.

FRIDAY NIGHT LIGHTS

Yes the word I got on Friday night was specific and powerful and yes it all came out exactly the way he said it would. He even told me I didn't know it, but that I was a preacher God was going to send all over the world. At that time, I had no notions of preaching, no ability to teach and had only left the state of Texas a handful of times. He told me to humble myself and love the people I was in court with because one day they would be called family.

Many of those people that I was in court with in 87 have been a big part of my ministry and church for years now. My youngest daughter wed an amazing young man in that wonderful family just this year and that word absolutely is coming to pass 25 years later.

With all that said, it was the presence of the Lord that truly changed my life that week. I fell in love with the author of that amazing book and he pounded a word into my life about advancement and progression.

The next several pages are an excerpt from my book titled *Numbers that preach*. It's all about this pattern of progression and what the number three tends to represent.

I do not believe there is any power in numbers but I do believe that there is power in God's word and sometimes He stamps a number on something to preach a powerful message.

Here's what I am talking about.

THE NUMBER THREE
"PERFECT COMPLETION"
This number also has to do with fullness and being all the way complete.
Three is resurrection. It's the number that God stamps on divinity.

THIRD DAY GLORY
Besides being the name of my all-time favorite Christian band, it was on the <u>third day</u> that the earth <u>rose</u> up from out of the water. God was first beginning to preach back then in faith that later we would hear His incredible message. That was the original standard for what God would love to preach through the number three.

About 2000 years after Adam had fallen and 2000 years before Jesus was risen, God formed a covenant with a man named Abraham. The Lord threw an eternal wrench into Abraham's theology by commanding him to sacrifice his promised son and the joy of his life.

They went for a long journey when the Bible says,

Genesis 22:4
*Then on the third day Abraham lifted up his eyes,
and saw the place (of sacrifice) afar off.*

The place of sacrifice that God showed him was not that far off in distance, it was far off in time. Nearly 2000 years in fact. Though it didn't have a name then, some later would call it Calvary and then others Golgotha. Not only did God show Abraham the place, but I believe he also saw the very sacrifice himself. Abraham lifted his eyes into the spirit and saw Jesus Christ laying down His life on the rugged cross for all of us. I know this because when Isaac asked where the sacrifice for the offering was, Abraham's reply was incredible.

Gen 22:8

And Abraham said, My son, God will provide himself
a lamb for a burnt offering:

Now when they got to the top of that mountain there was a ram
caught in a thicket and Abraham sacrificed him instead of Isaac.
But the Lamb that Abraham prophesied of would be provided
far off in the future by none other than God Himself. It was the
cup that Jesus drank from.

I showed you that to say this, not only did Abraham see the place
and see the person of the sacrifice, but he saw that He would be
resurrected as well! God's revelation to Abraham was preached
to him not on the first or the fourth day, but in fact as the Bible
says, on *the third day*.

FAST FORWARD
500 years later, Abraham's seed proliferated North Eastern Africa
like jack rabbits. In the third month after leaving the bondage of
Egypt, the Israelites arrived at the Sinai desert in droves. God
instructed Moses to tell the people to wash their clothes and to
be ready for the third day.

> *"for on the third day the Lord will come down on*
> *Mount Sinai before the eyes of all the people"*
> (Exod. 19:11).

God wanted to show everybody how awesome He was, not on
the first day, or even the seventh day, but of course on the third
day. He was preaching again.

About 1500 years later, the Lord would show the world how
incredible He really was by the resurrection of His son, not on
the 1st or the 4th day, but on the 3rd day.

The resurrection of Jesus has lots of threes around it because God was preaching that Jesus was the *perfectly complete* sacrifice for all time.

Jesus rose on the 3rd day
The writing on the cross was in three languages There were three crosses on Calvary
He was crucified on the third hour
There were three hours of darkness at Calvary
The last three words of Jesus were "It is finished"
Peter denied Jesus three times
(before the resurrection)
Peter acknowledged that he loved Jesus three times
(after the resurrection)

TRIPLE SEVENS

I have been to the traditional places in Israel that we think might be the place that Abraham saw afar off. It is interesting to note that Golgotha is said to be at exactly 777 feet above sea level (3 sevens).

It is fascinating to me to note that the famous man of the Shroud of Turin left a blood stain on his forehead in the form of a perfect three. I know the controversy over the authenticity of this ancient relic, but none the less, I 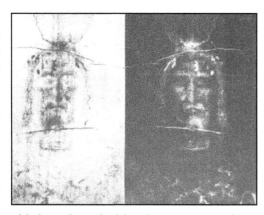 see God's watermark and it is written in blood. Do you see it?

Three is resurrection and there are those that believe this print was made at the resurrection of Jesus.

FULL OF THREES

Three is also the number of perfect completion and fullness.

Colossians 2:9
For in him dwelleth all the fullness of the Godhead bodily.

Even the word "fullness" occurs three times in the Bible.

Ephesians 3:19   Ephesians 4:13 Colossians 2:9
The fullness of God, the fullness of Christ and
the fullness of the Godhead.

That pretty much wraps up Jesus and there is a good chance that the Shroud of Turin did as well.

People that follow Jesus are called Christians. It is no coincidence that the word "Christian" appears only three times in the Bible:

Acts 11:26; 26:28; 1 Peter 4:16.

The reason being is because in Christ, Christians are full and we have the promise of resurrection stamped upon us.

Michael Hoggard points out that the term "born again" is found exactly three times in scripture and each time there is a reference to 3 either in chapter or in verse.

John 3:3
Jesus answered and said unto him, Verily, verily, I say unto thee, Except a man be born again, he cannot see the kingdom of God.

John 3:7
Marvel not that I said unto thee, Ye must be born again.

1 Peter 1: 23
Being born again, not of corruptible seed, but of incorruptible, by the word of God, which liveth and abideth forever.

His books "By Devine Order" and "The King James Code" make these kind of excellent points over and over again. He is also very good at pointing out that this only works in the King James Version, as the newer translations or commentaries tend to lose the numerical value all together.

THREE TO GET READY
Samson lied to Delilah three times before he revealed to her the source of his strength. When he did, his demise was complete. (Jud. 16:15).

Isaiah mentions three times that the wicked will have no peace (Isa. 48:22, 57:21, 59:8).

In Gen. 15:9, the Lord requests "a three-year-old heifer, a three-year-old she-goat and a three-year-old ram, because he can't stand things done half way.

Jesus raised three people from the dead
Three people in the Old Testament were resurrected
God spoke from Heaven three times
After Paul met Jesus, he was blind for three days
The Jordan River was parted 3 times
Noah's ark had three levels in it
God told Joshua three times to be courageous
Jonah was in the belly of the great fish 3 days

So "three" is the number that God uses to preach the perfect, complete fullness of something.

THREE AND THE NEXT LEVEL
The yellow brick road to God's greater things is a specific path of progression. What I am about to tell you goes against the grain of every fiber of our fast food generation.

God is a God of process.

Yes, there is a process God takes us through, and we have to concede & submit to this very important fact of life.

For God to perfectly complete that process in every area of our life, He likes to take us through THREE different stages. He illustrates this principle in "threes" throughout His Word.

FAST FOOD FAITH

The church today does not want to hear about process. In this fast food generation, we tend to contemplate everything with a microwave mentality. Instead of looking at Jesus as KING and receiving our marching orders, it seems the church today speaks to God like a demand at a drive through menu.

"Hold the pickles, hold the lettuce special orders don't upset us."

I see it in church all the time. Instead of Christians wanting to be a part of a fellowship of committed believers that is following Jesus and actively loving on a very lost world, they look for a quick action bless me center. It's easy to spot these fast-food junkies, because they are always couch potatoes. Words like commitment and faithfulness mean nothing to them. They want to be pew sitters and it had better be a cushioned pew in an air conditioned room. They quickly make their demands and as soon as they do not get what they ordered, they drive off and we never see them again.

"I'll take a pre-trib rapture, with a mixed praise and worship, and hold the speaking in tongues, please."

Like it or not, if you want to go on into His promises for your life, you are going to have to be willing to go through some things on your way there. There are no quick fixes or get rich quick schemes in God's plan. You are going to have to swallow some things that you didn't order. You are going to have to endure some long waits. You are going to have to hold your head together in the midst of sorry service.

Hebrews 6:15
And so, after he (Abraham) had patiently endured, he obtained the promise.

Christians that are into spiritual fast-food and playgrounds will remain in a wilderness experience with God. They may have gotten out of Egypt by the skin of their teeth and the blood of the Lamb, but they will never see the awesome promises of God fulfilled in their wandering lives. They will never see God's 3rd stage.

A GUT FOR HIS GLORY
If you can stomach the process there is a monster payoff that most people only dream about. You can see it in biblical terms of the Promised Land, or the most holy place within the temple. Perhaps you recognize this principle in Joseph's journey into Pharaoh's court or maybe you have seen a glimpse of how this works from reading about the jump from 30 to 60 and then to 100 fold in Mark chapter four.

However you want to pen it, we are talking about the realization of God's specific plan, purpose and yes, promises for your life. There is something much better for you and the Word clearly shows you how to get it, if you will let God preach His number three message.

THIRD STAGE
God does not perfectly complete anything without 3 different phases or stages.

The Bible gives an untold number of examples on how God takes us from EGYPT to the WILDERNESS and then to the PROMISED LAND.

For the people of God that are being led by the good, great and chief Shepherd, it is a guaranteed fact that Jesus Christ will take you from one stage to another stage in every area of your life. If you stop progressing, it is not because He stopped leading you into better things.

Isa 9:7
Of the increase of his government and
peace there shall be no end, ...

Nobody just wakes up and finds themselves in the midst of God's promises for their lives. There is a process involved. If you see any godly person's glory, don't forget to check out their story. There never has been, nor will there ever be, a great man or woman of God without going through great affliction.

That process is revealed as three different stages or phases that you go through, before the whole thing is accomplished or complete. These three stages are three different arenas where God deals with you in three levels. The reason for this is not that God changes from stage to stage, but that you change from stage to stage. Not only is this the reason, but this is the whole point of the process. We are supposed to change from one image into another.
Within those three stages there are lots of things that have to be accomplished within us before we can go on to the next stage. By knowing what these truths are, you can begin to map out where you are at and what has to be accomplished in order for you get to the next level. Nobody gets into the best that God has for them without going through all three stages.

The following is a collection of notes I have kept for more than twenty years. As I see the threes in scripture, I have kept them on scribbled notes in a shoe box long before anybody had a notebook to type them out on.

Here we go.

EXAMPLES OF THREE IN THE SCRIPTURE

God
Father   Son   Holy Spirit

Man
Body   Soul   Spirit

The Enemy
The Flesh   The World   The Devil

Time
Past   Present   Future

The Word of God
Written   Spoken   Living

The Temple
Outer Court   Inner Court   Most Holy Place

God Established His Covenant Through
Abraham   Isaac   Jacob

Jesus' Journey
Death   Burial   Resurrection

Joseph's Journey
Potipher's House   Prison   Pharaoh's Court

The Heavens
Sun   Moon   Stars

The Monarchy of Israel
Saul   David   Solomon

God's Covenant with Man
Law   Grace   Glory

The Exodus of Israel
Egypt   Wilderness   Promised Land

Moses
40 years as an Egyptian   40 years as a Shepherd
40 years as a Deliverer

The 3 Closest Disciples
Peter   James   John

3 Hebrew Children
Shadrach   Meshach   Abednego

The Sons of Noah
Shem   Ham   Japheth

The Power of the Devil
Accuse   Deceive   Condemn

God's Provision
Temporary   Daily   Permanent

Learning
Knowledge   Understanding   Wisdom
Acts 2:22
Signs   Miracles   Wonders

Revelation 2:2
Works   Labor   Patience

Revelation 17:14
Called   Chosen   Faithful

The Handiwork of God
1 Cor 3:12
Gold   Silver   Precious Stones

The Handiwork of Man
1 Cor 3:12
Wood   Hay   Stubble

Dimensions
Rev 21:16
Length   Breadth   Height

The Feasts
Deut 16:16
Unleavened Bread   Weeks   Tabernacles

The Levitical Priesthood
Levites   Priests   High Priest

The Three Different Arks
Noah's   Bulrushes   Covenant

The Contents of the Ark of the Covenant
Heb 9:4
Tablets   Aaron's Rod   Golden Pot

Acts 2:17
Prophecy   Visions   Dreams

Now Abideth
1 Cor 13:13
Faith   Hope   Love

God's Path
Proverbs 2:9 & 1:3
Righteousness   Judgment   Equity

The Way of the Flesh
1 John 2:16
Lust of the Flesh   Lust of the Eyes   Pride of Life

The Way of the World
Jude 1:11
Way of Cain   Error of Balaam
Gainsaying of Korah

The Great Commission
Mark 16:25
Go   Preach   Baptize

The Harvest
Matthew 4
30 fold   60 fold   100 fold

Temptation
James 1:15
Lust   Sin   Death

The Writing on the Wall
Daniel 5:25
Mene   Tekel   Peres

The Judgment of the Writing
Dan 5:25
Numbered   Weighed   Divided

The Judgments in Revelation
Seals   Trumpets   Vials

God Has Prepared a
2 Chr 6:38
Land   City   House

The Earth in Geneses 1
Without Form   Void
Darkness Was on the Face of the Deep

The Will of God
Romans 12:2
Good   Acceptable   Perfect

Jesus is Seen as a
John 7:40   Hebrews 3:1   1 Tim 6:15
Prophet   Priest   King

God is Our
Isaiah 33:22
Judge   Lawgiver   King

The Law
Deuteronomy 8:11
Commandments   Judgments   Statutes

The Weightier Things of the Law
Matthew 23:23
Judgment   Mercy   Faith

Jesus is
John 14:6
The Way   The Truth   The Life

Jesus is the
John 10:11 Hebrews 13:20 1 Peter 5:4
Good Shepherd Great Shepherd Chief Shepherd

Responsibility of the Seeker
Matthew 7:7
Ask Seek Knock

Men are
2 Cor 7:2
Wronged Corrupted Defrauded
By Religion

Mary at the Feet of Jesus
Luke 7:44
Washed Kissed Anointed

They Came to Take Jesus With
John 18:3
Lanterns Torches Weapons

3 Gifts Brought to Jesus
Matthew 2:11
Gold Frankincense Myrrh

Humility
Eph 4:2
Lowliness Meekness Long-suffering

The Bible Was Written in 3 Original Languages Hebrew
Aramaic Greek

God Made Language Itself to Have 3 Degrees
Positive Comparative Superlative

3 Ways Daniel Sought God With
Dan 9:3
Fasting   Sackcloth   Ashes

David Was Anointed 3 Times By
Samuel   The Men of Judah
The Elders of Jerusalem

We Honor Jesus by Receiving
Matthew 10
Prophets   Righteous Men   Children

The Baptism of
Matthew 3:11
Repentance   Holy Ghost   Fire

In the Last Days Many Will
Matt 24:10
Be Offended   Betray   Hate

3 Witnesses of God's Grace
1 John 5:7
The Spirit   The Water   The Blood

In Christ We Have Been
Baptized   Buried   Planted
Romans 6: 3, 4 & 5

The 5 offices in Eph 4:11 Are For
The Perfecting of the Saints
The Work of the Ministry
The Edifying of the Body of Christ.

Romans 14:17
Righteousness   Peace   Joy

Our relationship with God
Servants   Friends   Sons

God is bringing us into perfect completion. Each time He reveals that message, He loves to stamp the number 3 on it.

Everything I just showed you is taking place on the 3rd planet in our solar system and is being revealed by the 3rd part of the Godhead known as the Holy Ghost. Did I mention that the phrase "Holy Ghost" is found 90 times (30 x 3) in the Bible?

THE SUM OF ALL THINGS THREE
Can you see the progression and the three different stages of progression in all of the patterns? There are actually many more than just the ones I have listed.

I want to ask you, are you a thirty fold Christian like what Jesus talks about in Matthew 13? Or, do you fall into that rare group of 60 fold Christianity or maybe even the endangered species of the 100 fold Christians?

Are you with the masses in the outer Court or will you progress all the way into the most holy place.

Are you still living in Egypt as most Christians are, seeing yourself as a slave or have you moved out into the wilderness and found that you are the friend of God? Better yet, are you one of the rare people who are into relationship with God as a son and move into the promised land? You do know that friends don't receive the inheritance and that's why Moses never entered in. Only sons of God receive his inheritance.

The Pattern of progression that the bible takes us through typically comes in three different stages.

I declare in Jesus name that you are not only going to see the first stage but all three, right here in the land of the living.

What an amazing journey you are on!

_____
_____
_____
_____
_____
_____
_____
_____
_____
_____
_____
_____
_____
_____
_____
_____
_____
_____

Three is also the number of perfect completion and fullness.

Colossians 2:9
For in him dwelleth all the fullness of the Godhead bodily.

"Even the word "fullness" occurs three times in the Bible. Ephesians 3:19, Ephesians 4:13 & Colossians 2:9. The fullness of God, the fullness of Christ and the fullness of the Godhead." Troy Brewer : Living Life /Forward & Numbers That Preach

CHAPTER SEVEN

Jack has left the Box

The box of the universe gets bigger every day, outrunning our ability to discover the end of it. The design of the universe and all things created cause us to go to another level if we want to see further.

Think about how smart that design is. If you want to see further you have to change to a bigger lens. In other words, if you want to move /forward you have to be willing to change to however the next level demands.

HOW FAR THE RABIT HOLE GOES

An Oxford-trained lawyer-turned-astronomer named Edwin Hubble, looked through the smoke of his pipe and the 100 inch lens of a telescope to find the truth I just mentioned, way back in the 1920's.

Yet, nearly a hundred years later, a big part of the church seems suspicious of the idea that the heart and works of God have not fully yet been discovered.

I think this is because so much of the church is unwilling to change their own lens.

They don't know the Daniel prophecy that says in the last days the knowledge, I think of God, would greatly increase as people moved /forward from one place to another. (Daniel 12:4)

They haven't considered the prophet Habakkuk, or the meaning of his name, *"Embrace"* in grabbing onto the idea of a much deeper revelation of God to be found in the end times.

For the earth shall be filled with the knowledge of the glory of
the LORD, as the waters cover the sea.
Habakkuk 2:14

SWITCH!

Sometimes in order to go to the next level, we have to be willing
to change how we do things and how we think about things.
Sometimes, the change is so radical, it takes a special grace and
word from God to be able to deal with it. Sometimes the problem
is deeply rooted in our own identity and to what we think we
owe our allegiance to.

In Acts Chapter 10, the bible records an extraordinary vision with
an extraordinary person. Peter, a man with strong nationalist, if
not racists' views, received a vision from God in which he saw
a table cloth coming down out of heaven. It was all about a feast
and on this table were "all kinds of four-footed animals of the
earth, wild beasts, creeping things, and birds of the air" (verse
12).

So there were things he would usually eat and there were also
bugs and all kinds of things he usually would not eat. Most
notably were things on this table that the old covenant and all of
Jewish culture would never eat.

A voice from God then exhorted Peter to "kill and eat" (verse
13), to which Peter objected that he had never eaten anything
"common" (koinos in Greek) or "unclean" (akathartos in Greek).

The first word refers to animals that had not been bled
appropriately or had died of themselves. It makes me wonder if
in this Holy Ghost buffet was some kind of road kill.

The second is the word used to refer to the unclean animals in
Leviticus 11 and Deuteronomy 14.

Peter reacted to both in the same way.
The King James' boys translate his objection as,
> *"Not so, Lord!"*

Another translation says,
> *"Surely not Lord!"*

Another translation says,
> *"By no means, Lord!"*

If I was to translate it, I think I would put it this way,

> *"You're smoking crack, Lord!*

It had never entered into Peter's mind that God could call an unclean animal clean, much less an uncircumcised Roman, or a common Texan, saved.

The voice of God that Peter loved so much, was saying something very different than he had ever heard.

God then told him, "What God has cleansed you must not call common" (verse 15).

The key to understanding this event is in verse 28, where Peter explains: *"You know how unlawful it is for a Jewish man to keep company with or go to one of another nation. But God has shown me that I should not call any man common or unclean"*

This went very much against the grain and decision making paradigm for any Jew of the first century, much less a zealot like Peter. As far as they knew, they were the only nation God was working with.

So, prior to the conversion of the entire household of the Roman centurion Cornelius in Acts 10:17-48, the apostle Peter had to receive a life changing switch if he was ever going to go /forward.

This was the same revelation Isaiah had come to in chapter 6 of his prophetic book. God is able to make clean anybody even if he is from an unclean people!

God wanted Peter to be a vital part of the next big step and Peter had to change everything in order to be a part of it.

THE LONG AND WINDING ROAD

Everybody wants an upgrade but most of us can't handle a quick upgrade. There are several places in the bible that indicate sometimes everything changes in a moment, in a twinkling of an eye or on "That day."

The difference between the long and winding road that the beetles sang about and the *suddenlys* that can happen for all of us, has to do with our willingness to change.

Notice what Paul says about the famous day that everything changes from temporal to eternal.

> *in a moment, in the twinkling of an eye, at the last trump:*
> *for the trumpet shall sound, and the dead shall be raised*
> *incorruptible, and we shall be changed*
> 1 Cor 15:52

The greatest suddenly and upgrade of all, known as the rapture of the church, takes place and instantly God miraculously gives us the grace to change.

> *After these things I looked, and behold, a door standing open*
> *in heaven, and the first voice which I had heard, like the sound*
> *of a trumpet speaking with me, said, "Come up here...*
> Revelation 4:1

There is no going up miraculously, without a miraculous change on our parts. You wanna go up? You gotta change.

THE CHANGE OF LIFE
Saul reigned as King for 40 years as did David and Solomon. The first three Kings of Israel's monarchy, show the difference our willingness to change can make in the calling for upgrade God has given us.

Saul was instantly made King but when things happen quickly you have to surrender your heart to God quickly and that never really happened with Saul.

He was invited into a radical upgrade that required a radical change on his part. He was willing to accept the upgrade, you know, the best house in the country, the most beautiful women in your race, the mightiest warriors at your disposal, power, riches etc. However, he was not willing to conform his life to the image of that upgrade and it cost him his empire, his family and even his life.

EARLY TO RISE
See most people can't handle a fast rise to the top because instant change is required.

This is where the reality of upgrade and /forward
comes crashing into the responsibility we each carry with miraculous things.

It is one thing for God to reveal his wonderful plan for you. It is a whole other thing for you to conform your life to the image of that plan.

Saul was King in title but not in heart, so God went after a man who was after God's own heart. David was willing to go through a terribly difficult process of conforming his life to look like the image of God's plan, way before he ever saw it manifest.

Saul was exactly opposite and ended up begging for death on the bloody slopes of Gilboa. It wasn't his upgrade that killed him, it was his inability to change once the upgrade happened that killed him. There was a whole new life of responsibilities required of him, he never owned up to.

THE STORY OF THE GLORY
My daughter Meagan has wanted to be a nurse since she was little bitty.

"When I grow up I want to be a nurse so I can wear a white suit." she said to my wife when she was only four.

Her grandmother and several of her aunts are nurses and sure enough, today she is a full blown R.N.

She serves the Lord and the people she helps in living out her dream at a hospital in Ft Worth.

In order for Meagan to realize her God given dream, she had to go through the incredibly difficult process of making that happen.

Meagan never loved school but she had to make herself conform to the image of that plan. She never knew how to apply for grants but she had to be willing to wrap her head around those uncomfortable things and get good at making it work.

She had never driven in Dallas and had to become skilled at moving around that big city. She had to work a full time job while going to school full time. She had the difficulty of social issues of a young, beautiful woman in her twenties. She had to navigate through financial issues, spiritual issues and tons of other things. All the while, learning to work with her professors and doctors and moving in the culture of the medical field. The process she went through made her somebody who makes it look easy to do what she does now.

You see her glory but not her story.

IT'S BEST TO BE BLESSED
It takes hard work and commitment to be blessed. It takes selflessness and a willing to change what you like and what you do not like or who you like to move /forward.

People who walk in the promises of God are people who have been through difficult things to get there. Just because they do not smell like smoke, doesn't mean they have been through the fire.

...and the king's counselors, being gathered together, saw these men, upon whose bodies the fire had no power, nor was a hair of their head singed, neither were their coats affected, nor had the smell of fire come upon them
Daniel 3:27

Even though it looks painless, to change something and make it conform to something it has never been, tends to hurt. We learn not to give in to pain and discomfort because we know God is our rewarder and when the reward comes you forget the pain.

A woman, when she gives birth, has sorrow, because her time has come. But when she has delivered the child, she doesn't remember the anguish any more, for the joy that a human being is born into the world
John 16:21

When we refuse to *yield our members* (Romans 6:13) and conform our lives to the heart and dreams of God, we forfeit our upgrade to another.

> *And Samuel said to (Saul), The LORD has torn the kingdom of*
> *Israel from you this day, and has given it to a*
> *neighbor of yours, who is better than you.*
> 1st Samuel 15:28

A simple but sober understanding of how this works can help us get out of our box and into a better place.

BREAKING THE BOX

/Forward for all of us is not in the confines of what we are used to. We have to learn, pursue and conform.

It will require you to work with teams when you are an individualist and go through things alone when you wish you could party with your friends.

It will require you to lay down what you think is a big deal and re-prioritize what you haven't really cared about before.

If you are going to do that thing, God says you have to be willing to be that guy. In fact he already says that you are that guy, YOU just have to chisel away the parts that don't look like him.

GOD THOUGHTS AND MEDITATIONS

Do not hate the process of laying things down and picking things up according to what God requires. It's wisdom. It's what Saul rejected and Solomon asked for and a huge part of your ongoing move into better.

"The difference between the long and winding road that the beetles sang about and the *suddenlys* that can happen for all of us, has to do with our willingness to change."
Troy Brewer : Living Life /Forward

CHAPTER EIGHT

The Pursuit of Happiness

The "American Dream" is one of the most commonly misunderstood ideas in American culture. Stephen Stone in his article, *the dying American dream*, wrote something I think is worth reading;

"The term is used loosely to mean just about anything from the acquisition of wealth, to home ownership, to moral license, to success in court against McDonald's--all without appreciation for the original significance of the Dream. Because the American Dream is largely misunderstood, as well as taken for granted, it is in danger of disappearing altogether."

I like what He had to say a decade ago and it seems much more amplified now. The purpose of the United States constitution is not to guarantee a dream to anybody, but to guarantee the opportunity for Americans to pursue that dream. There is a big kingdom principle of /forward in this.

I DECLARE

"Life, Liberty and the pursuit of Happiness" is a well-known phrase in the United States Declaration of Independence and considered by some as part of one of the most well-crafted, influential sentences in the history of the English language. These words are anointed and God breathed and if you think that's hokey, well rain on you.

When the 55 signers wrote their "John Hancock" under the 55 words of declaration, they handed themselves a place of honor in America's history and a death warrant by the British government.

In their minds, the right to pursue one's own heart and dreams, outside of government shackles was so essential, they were willing to die for it.

THE PURSUIT THAT GOD BLESSES
God does not bless the chosen frozen on their blessed assurance. God blesses pursuit.

The only finders in this Kingdom are seekers. The only people who get the answers in this Kingdom are the people who consistently ask. The people who walk through supernatural doors into powerful upgrades are the ones willing to go to the door and knock until somebody finally answers.

Limp wristed attitudes in the kingdom produce weak results. The inventor of life is first a loving father, but don't forget He is also a Warrior King.

You have to go after it. Against the odds, against what's accepted as normal. Against what makes sense, you have to be willing to pursue what is on your heart before God can bless it!

MAKING TRACKS
In the arena of promised-land living, you never see what God has given you until you are willing to walk in it first. In the promised land you have to be willing to walk in it before you get it.

Every place where you set your foot will be yours:
Your territory will extend from the desert to Lebanon,
and from the Euphrates River to the western sea.
Deuteronomy 11:24

When God told Joshua to cross the flooded Jordan River and go into the Promised Land, he did something very different than when they left Egypt to cross over into the wilderness. Both

involved miraculous crossings of bodies of water. Who can
forget about Moses and the crossing of the red sea?

But here at the gateway to the Promised Land, a different courage
and trust is required as the key. The water didn't part first like
it did when they moved from Egypt into the wilderness. This
was the Promised Land, and there were a new set of rules. They
had to start pursuing the Promised Land *before* the waters ever
parted.

*It was the harvest season, and the Jordan was overflowing its
banks. But as soon as the feet of the priests who were carrying
the Ark touched the water at the river's edge, the water above
that point began backing up a great distance away at a town
called Adam, which is near Zarethan. And the water below that
point flowed on to the Dead Sea until the riverbed was dry.
Then all the people crossed over near the town of Jericho.*
Joshua 3:15 and 16

In this arena, the way does not present itself until you move
towards it. You have to step in it first.

LESSONS FROM THE WILDERNESS
As already discussed in my first chapter, the lesson of the
wilderness is that God protects those who stay close to Him
no matter what. God stayed in front of the people as a cloud
by day and fire by night. They followed, never knowing where
they were going and the only strategy they were allowed was a
strategy of day to day survival which meant sticking close to the
goodness of God.

We have to learn those lessons and live those lessons but let me
tell you this.

THE LESSON OF THE PROMISED LAND
IS THAT GOD BLESSES PURSUIT

The Promised Land is different. Through God given strategy and courage they took on walled cities, 31 kingdoms and warrior giants. In the wilderness you follow the Lord and survive but in the Promised Land you follow Vision and God backs you up.

In the wilderness He says, "Follow me and I will make a way." In the Promised Land He says, you make a way and I will back you up."

In the wilderness the miracle is that you are fed manna from heaven and water from rocks. In the Promised Land, provision is never the issue, the miracle happens in pursuit of conquest.

Consider the difference in relationship between the two places of the wilderness and the Promised Land

Then the manna ceased on the day after they had eaten the produce of the land; and the children of Israel no longer had manna, but they ate the food of the land of Canaan that year.
Joshua 5:12

They moved from miraculous provision to miraculous exploits of winning battles. The wilderness is full of slaves learning to become God's people. The Promised Land is full of God's people learning to be warriors who accomplish great vision.

So where do you want to live?

DRESSED TO KILL
In the early nineties I was preparing to leave for a mission's trip to New Orleans. My wife had dropped me off at a Pastor's house whose name was James (*I feel God*) Brown.

When he came to the door, he hugged me and invited me in saying, "Please excuse our mess, my wife done lost her mind."

"No problem", I said but I seriously wondered what he was talking about.

Inside the house everything was packed up into boxes, ready for a big move. There were boxes everywhere from one end to the other.

"Ya'll are about to move, where you moving to?" I sheepishly asked.

"We don't know." said Pastor Brown

"My wife has been praying for a new house in a better neighborhood and last week she got a word it was all about to happen. So this week, she packed it all up and said, God has a new house for me."

 We both busted out laughing and began making proclamations of a better home. That was the last time I ever went to that house because not long after she got a big upgrade and her prayer was answered.

I don't know very many people who would pack up before they knew where they were going but this lady did.

God loves that. So...guess what He did?

THE HOUND OF HEAVEN
We need to follow the example of our Lord in being what C.S. Lewis calls *the hound of Heaven*. He has chased us and pursued us. He called us blessed and holy before we were even saved. He said we were His before we ever cared anything about Him.

What I mean is this, if you think you are called to go on a missions trip, don't wait until you have the money to go after it.

Get a passport. Study the nations. Learn a new language. Get your shots. Prepare gifts, do whatever you can to step into the territory that God has given you.

Oh, that makes God happy!

If you are called to write a book, get a Mac or some other inferior word processor. I'm smiling.

Write a newspaper column and send it in to your local newspaper. Read the kinds of books that you would like to write and study how the book is written.

Take an on line course or two on writing. Go to some book signings and get acquainted with authors.

Join a book witting club or at least some blog sites. Pursue! Put the soles of your feet in contact with the place God has given you and He will make it yours!

MAPPED OUT MOMENTUM
The laws of momentum, which I have already mapped out, applies here. If you sit there and say, "I am helpless and can't make it," God has a wilderness for you where He will love you and help you to be a survivor.

Instead of saying amen, say Yikes.

But if you trust in Him and go after your passion He will empower you with supernatural abilities to accomplish vision and He will make you an overcomer!

GOD THOUGHTS AND MEDITATIONS ON MOMENTUM

_____
_____
_____
_____
_____
_____
_____
_____
_____
_____
_____
_____
_____
_____
_____
_____
_____
_____
_____
_____
_____
_____

Every place where you set your foot will be yours: Your territory will extend from the desert to Lebanon, and from the Euphrates River to the western sea.
Deuteronomy 11:24

"In the Wilderness He says, "Follow me and I will make a way." In the promised land He says, You make a way and I will back you up."
Troy Brewer : Living Life /Forward

CHAPTER NINE
Paying the Price for /Forward

Yes, there is a price and if the price is right, you could get the deal of the century. Here we go.

LET'S MAKE A DEAL
The Largest land deal in history made the United States twice as big at the stroke of a pen and the raising of a flag. The Louisiana Purchase was made in 1803 and the United States paid approximately $15 million dollars for over 800,000 square miles of land.

Today we know Louisiana as the little state just east of Texas full of swamps, gators, Cajuns, Jazz music and casinos. What Thomas Jefferson actually bought was a territory of virtually everything west of known America.

To Jefferson, Louisiana meant the next place for /forward. If he didn't take the next step, the North American continent would not be filled with the lower 48 states but would eventually become Western Europe.

Whether or not America had a *'Manifest Destiny'* to span from 'sea to sea' as was often the rallying cry of the early to mid-19th century, the desire for this territory could not be denied by Jefferson.

If there was ever the right President at the right time to have such a vision, it was he. His deal was arguably the greatest achievement of Thomas Jefferson's presidency for many different reasons but there is one reason I want to especially point out.

THE PRICE FOR DISCOVERY

Thomas Jefferson paid a huge price, money he didn't have and had to borrow from England at 6% interest. The incredible price he paid was not for something he could show to anybody, but something which had to be discovered.

The boundaries were not even defined because Meriwether Lewis and William Clark had not yet led a small expeditionary group called the Corps of Discovery, into the territory.

Do you understand that the Louisiana Purchase was made before anybody even knew what it was? The United States went /forward because somebody was willing to pay the price for something still yet undiscovered.

Jefferson paid a terrible price for something he could not even define to anybody because He knew he had to go there. It just was not an option for America to remain the way it was.

Can you do that? Can you pay a big price for something that is not even mapped out yet? Can you sell out for something simply because you do not have the option to remain where you are?

If you can, I promise you, you will get your upgrade. All of Heaven is ready to applaud your rare courage and our amazing vision for bigger and better.

During peace time, can you do something incredibly uncomfortable for the vision of something much greater?

Can you dedicate all you have to something you don't even know how to define yet?

Thomas Jefferson did and we all are blessed because of it. So did Abraham by the way.

The Lord said to Abram:
Leave your country, your family, and your relatives and go to
the land that I will show you. I will bless you and make your
descendants into a great nation.

You will become famous and be a blessing to others. I will
bless anyone who blesses you, but I will put a curse on anyone
who puts a curse on you. Everyone on earth will be blessed
because of you.

Abram was seventy-five years old when the Lord told him to
leave the city of Haran. He obeyed and left with his wife Sarai,
his nephew Lot, and all the possessions and slaves they had
gotten while in Haran.

When they came to the land of Canaan, Abram went as far as the
sacred tree of Moreh in a place called Shechem. The Canaanites
were still living in the land at that time, but the Lord appeared
to Abram and promised, "I will give this land to your family
forever." Abram then built an altar there for the Lord.
Genesis 12:1-7
Contemporary English Version The Holy Bible

A Land That I Will Show You...Later. Really?

Oh Yes. See, that's God.

I have thought a lot about Abram's call to /forward. I wonder
what that conversation must of went like when He told his
family he was leaving.

"Mom, dad, I'm leaving everything I know and all the security
of my future."

"Why?"

"Because God came to me and told me to."

"What God? What is His name?"

"He didn't tell me but I trust His voice."

"Well why do you have to leave to follow him?"

"I don't know He didn't say. He just promised I would be blessed."

"But you are already blessed. Where is this God taking you to for this great blessing?"

"I don't know dad, some place He said He would personally show me, ...later."

UNEXPLAINABLE AND UNDENIABLE
I could spend a hundred pages on this one chapter but let's get straight to the point.

In the Kingdom, it is often the case that we know something before we know how to define it. This is perfectly normal for people who have a heart after God's own heart.

From the very beginning, God has called people of faith to move towards things that were not fully mapped out for them.

While the cerebrally faithless, who call themselves "*watchmen on the walls*", sit in contempt of anybody who runs with God, there are others living unexplainable lives.

The fever for /forward comes with a big appetite for the unexplainable and the indescribable. The romantic notion of "*mystery and adventure*" comes coupled with the hard rock assurance of God given vision and strategy.

I have already said, if you can explain everything God is doing in your life, your walk in Jesus is way too safe and shallow.

So don't wait for you to have it all mapped out before you start walking in it. Just know that it is God and let that be enough for you.

This is how God prepares us to have a heart that says yes, -before we even know what the next command is.

A PIONEER SPIRIT
God blesses a heart and a life that is willing to explore.

Most Christians never move out of Egypt or past the outer court and see past the sun when there is still the moon and the stars to explore.

When you decide to accept the invitation to upgrade you have to set your heart on a whole new dial.

Blessed are those whose strength is in you,
who have set their hearts on pilgrimage
Psalms 84:5

GOD THOUGHTS AND MEDITATIONS
ON BEING A PIONEER

A heart set on pilgrimage is one that is willing to explore, not one
that is wanting to play it safe. A Kingdom pilgrim finds strength
in the Lord not in familiar situations and circumstances.

_____
_____
_____
_____
_____
_____
_____
_____
_____
_____
_____
_____
_____
_____
_____
_____

Blessed are those whose strength is in you,
who have set their hearts on pilgrimage
Psalms 84:5

"Can you do that? Can you pay a big price for something that is
not even mapped out yet? Can you sell out for something simply
because you do not have the option to remain where you are?"
Troy Brewer : Living Life /Forward

SECTION THREE
The way through the wilderness

Henry Frapp: I thought you got lost again.
Nathan Wyeth: Haven't you ever been lost?
Henry Frapp: Hmmm... been fearsome confused for a month or two, but I ain't never been lost.

THE MOUNTAIN MEN, 1980

CHAPTER TEN
The Lessons of the wilderness

Ok, let's take a break for a moment and get into something that is absolutely essential to /Forward Life Living. If this book were a song this section would be the bridge that departs from the chorus and brings the whole thing back together again.

I want to talk to you about a door that is not very good looking but one you will have to go through. For you to live life /forward you will have to be very familiar with a very unattractive part of your amazing upgrade. It's a really wild place that takes a while to get used to.

The wilderness is ugly. Nobody likes the wilderness. It's harsh, uncomfortable and avoided by everybody who is smart enough to read a map. The wilderness is all about survival. Nobody, at first, looks /forward to a fight for his life but we all find ourselves in that ring in different parts of our lives at different times of our lives.

But there is something in the wilderness you have to see for yourself. Something that can only be found there and no place else. I want to tell you about it because you are going to go through the wilderness many different times in your life and I want to help you make your discovery.

It is important, in fact essential to your legacy, that you go *through* the wilderness and not just *to* the wilderness.

God doesn't want you to stay in the wilderness, He wants you learn how to stay totally dependent upon Him. He wants you to be convinced that He is greater than anything *Egypt* can offer you.

It's in that place where you hear Him like never before. He has amazing things to tell you that you will never know unless He personally tells you, and we learn that part of God in the wilderness.

The Door to your next level is in the place your bible describes as a wilderness. It's the last place you would think you would go to move /forward but it's the only place you can go to if you really what an upgrade.

The Wilderness is not beautiful but God is.

A lot of people never make it out of those ugly, harsh places they have to journey through. There are better and smarter people than you and I that have failed miserably, lost marriages, ministries, even their lives because they could not get through the wilderness-but you will.

I know you will.

Because what you discover in the wilderness will not only get you out of the wilderness, it will get the enemy out of your promised land.

It is in the wilderness you discover how awesome God is to you and how precious you are to Him. Let's do this.

THE LONE STAR OF DAVID
Until recently, I thought the ugliest place on the planet was Monahan Texas. West Texas has some of the greatest people on the planet but Monahan makes Rodney Dangerfield look like Brad Pitt.

Recently, I have seen a place much, much worse and I have been reading about it in my bible for years and years. The Biblical wilderness is something difficult to describe and easy to understand by personal experience. It's ugly.

A month ago, Leanna and I went to Israel with a magnificent teacher named Dr. John Turner and a big part of our Journey was south of Jerusalem on the Egyptian border.

There are places in the wilderness you can see 50 miles in every direction and not see a single tree. Nothing but black rock, with its high iron content burnt by the roasting sun, sand and more rock. No water, nothing green, no wildlife.

Everything about the wilderness screams at you, "You will certainly die alone in this place." and it's hard not to believe the wilderness when it tells you that.

Now I physically spent my first time in the biblical wilderness last month, but it was not the first time I had a wilderness experience.

THE WILDERNESS YOU KNOW
You know that place even though you may have never stomped around in the middle east. You know what it is like to find yourself in an ugly place where it is easy to be overwhelmed by this harsh environment.

Like you, I have been in ugly places where I thought those places would do me in. I have wandered in seasons of my life without a map or even language to define where I was at or how I was going to make it. That's the wilderness.

You don't have to go to Israel to go to the wilderness. You don't have to make God mad to go to the Wilderness. You just have to live long enough and you will end up there.

Nobody moves /forward and avoids the wilderness. Nobody.

Jesus Himself was immediately led by the Spirit into the Wilderness just right after The Father announced how pleased He was with Him. So you see, the wilderness is not the place God sends you to show you He is mad at you. The wilderness is the place where He speaks an upgrade into your life that changes everything and brings you into the place of promise.

WHAT IT LOOKS LIKE
The wilderness is the place where everything you have known as life is no longer seen. It's the place you go that you have always feared. It's the place where you have no plan because everything has changed and you don't know how to get out of the place you are in.

I could go on but let me tell you something. The wilderness is not the place where you are supposed to live. It's the place you go through so you can live a life more abundantly in the Promises God has given you.

It's the in-between-place like the white part of an Oreo cookie. It's the place between the place where you were and the place where you are going.

It's the place between Egypt and the Promised land. The place where you transition from being owned to owning and from being conquered to being more than a conqueror. -And just like the white part of an Oreo cookie, it's actually the best part.

God Causes His goodness to pass before us in the Wilderness and He changes us from slaves to warriors. From Outcasts to His kids.

There is no way I could write a book about Kingdom principles of moving /forward without a discussion of the wilderness.

PREDETERMINED BEHAVIOR

How we behave in our wilderness experiences determines if we are qualified for the next level.

There are lessons and experiences you must gain in the wilderness absolutely essential to your next level. My friend John Turner said something amazing while we were there. "While the wilderness is not intended to be permanent, its lessons should be."

Let's map some of that out.

WHAT THE HECK IS THAT?

Our fathers did eat manna in the desert; as it is written, He gave them bread from heaven to eat. John 6:31

The bible says that God caused something called manna to miraculously appear on the ground in the wilderness. The word Manna actually means "What is that?"

His provision in the wilderness is very difficult to put your finger on. The way God provides for you in these tough places doesn't look like the way He provides for you in other places. You don't really know how He does it, or what to compare it to. You just know that He is the provider and His provision is miraculous.

God's provision in the wilderness is indescribable.

I have had times in my life where I ended up on the long end of the stick instead of the short end and had no way to articulate how I had made it or how God had done it. That's manna in the wilderness.

In the wilderness we learn to be ok with the unexplainable. This is a big lesson we learn in the wilderness. God is the answer to everything we do not have an answer for.

In the wilderness, we learn to live unexplainable lives based on how good His heart is, instead of how well we have things figured out.

Methods do not mean as much in the wilderness and we learn to just trust God rather than what we have always trusted in and this becomes a core value in our life for the rest of our life.

THE POSITION OF YOUR CAMP

And the LORD spake unto Moses and unto Aaron, saying, Every man of the children of Israel shall pitch by his own standard, with the ensign of their father's house: far off about the tabernacle of the congregation shall they pitch. Numbers 2:1&2

In the wilderness your only job is to stay close to God. Everything in the wilderness is about you learning to move when God moves and to stand where God stands.

You set up camp based on the manifest presence of God in your life. (*Around the tabernacle when God shows up).*

For you and I, this means we learn how to live out our lives from the place where God lives with us.
We conform our lives to making it revolve around who God is to us. It is in the wilderness, that ugly place we wanted to avoid, where we learn how to do this.

We must learn how to live everyday life with the manifest presence of God and the place where God shows us how to live with him is in our wilderness experience.

If you get away from the cloud by day or the fire by night, the wilderness kills you, and you're not about to do that. You learn to love the presence of God in the wilderness. You learn to live at peace and in a state of rest even though we are in harsh circumstances, there.

All of this is training for the big move /forward that is headed your way. All of this is about learning to love intimacy with God and partnering with God.

THE WILDERNESS: A WHOLE NEW WAY OF DOING THINGS

A big part of your personality and the way you think and do things simply comes from the culture you grew up in.

Culture is simply "the way we do things."

Another big lesson we learn in the wilderness is to be directly influenced by God in how we act and think instead of the culture we have been embedded in.

In the wilderness we come out of the influences of the world we grew up in and personally learn from God what our priorities should be. We learn to do things differently and think about things differently from how we live with Him. I love the wilderness!

WHERE THE MOB DOESN'T RULE
I hate the mob.

It's the spirit of the roman coliseum. It is the Rodney King Riot in LA. It's the church board with a religious spirit.

The mob is the Christmas shopping season and six flags over Texas on any day in July. It's the highway on Labor Day weekend and the parking lot of Wal-Mart.

The mob is New Orleans at Mardi Gras and people will do things with a mob they would never do on their own. Things make since with the mob that shouldn't and what should make sense never does in the mob. There is no reasoning with the mob.

Whether its rush hour traffic or a family reunion, people act completely different in a mob of people and it is always ruled by carnal emotions.

There is no mob in the wilderness. God gets to rule the way He really wants to rule when you find Him in that place.

ROCK N ROLL MISSIONS TRIP
In 2012 my wife and I went on a missions trip to Sierra Leone, West Africa. The last day we were there, our bus driver decided to take a narrow market street as a short cut to the ferry. Our bus was wider than the road and the vendor's tables were actually blocking the flow of traffic. At some point, we accidentally ran over a vendor's table. Within moments our bus was surrounded by hundreds of vendors who were demanding justice and pounding on our windows! Our guide went outside the bus and physically began to fight for his own life as others began to pile onto our bus.

The mob got in such a frenzy and so violent, so quickly. As they rocked our bus back and forth, most had no idea what they were yelling at us about at all. They were just under the influence of a frenzied group of people.

God did a miracle and like a tornado, it ended just as abruptly as it had begun. Suddenly our bus was moving and we drove out of the crowd.

Every time we go into a wilderness experience, we are quickly drawn away from the influence of the loudest screaming voice in our midst. We are no longer under the influence of those around us or caught up in the current of things.

We learn to let God influence everything we do and even think while we are in the wilderness. A big point of the wilderness is really just about learning to get alone with Him and living life from that intimate experience.

COMMENTS FROM THE COMMITTEE

When Moses brought some million or more Jewish people out of 400 years of slavery, He took them straight to the Promised Land. That's what a good leader does.

In a spirit of plurality of leadership, he formed a committee of men to represent the congregation and spy out the Promised Land.

Then Moses sent them to spy out the land of Canaan, and said to them, "Go up this way into the South, and go up to the mountains, and see what the land is like: whether the people who dwell in it are strong or weak, few or many; whether the land they dwell in is good or bad; whether the cities they inhabit are like camps or strongholds; whether the land is rich or poor; and whether there are forests there or not. Be of good courage. And bring some of the fruit of the land." Numbers 13:17

He was asking them to evaluate the methods of how they should enter and to see what they were up against, but they came back with an argument about *if* they should enter at all.

In the name of accountability, they decided it safer to not go /forward and there you have the first board ran church. They were responsible alright; they were personally responsible for the death of an entire generation. -All in the name of accountability and safety. It was really all about their lack of belief and need to control.

Religion always falls back to doubt and control and they find credibility in the mob they tend to rally with their lies.

Most church boards have followed suit ever since.

A FLOCK OF BUZZARDS
If you tell me there is a biblical model for a committee ran ministry, I will agree. It's right there in the book of Numbers Chapter 13 and a mob of people can keep you from entering God's promises.

What Israel needed then is what most Christians need today, they need some alone time with God to get their heads and hearts right again.

Back to the wilderness they went.

In the wilderness, you are confronted with disposing of the mob that influences you away from Him and keeps you from your upgrade.

So God sent them into the wilderness. Moses needed the wilderness because the wilderness is the place you go to get away from the influence of the mob. The wilderness is the place you find yourself alone. Now catch this, the point is not for you to be alone, but to be alone with God.

ALONE AT LAST
God loves to take us to the wilderness because He gets to have His way with us there.

You don't find out how bad God is in the wilderness but to the contrary, you find out how good God is.

The wilderness humbles you and you welcome God's presence there. You long for Him, as the deer pants for the water.

You learn that God is your friend in the wilderness and you also learn the world is not. There, you know the world wants to kill you but God wants to give you life and all this happens when you come away with Him.

In spite of what the groups of doubters and haters say, you learn the safest place you can possibly be is next to the beating heart of God. You learn that in the wilderness.

So are you beginning to see why no one escapes the wilderness? Because there is no upgrade without an upgrade in relationship with Jesus. You can't escape an amazing encounter with Him if you really want to move /forward.

NATURALLY SUPERNATURAL
We learn that God does things supernaturally in the wilderness and it becomes a lifestyle for His people. We become naturally supernatural people who expect to see water come from rocks. We learn that God is not confined to anything in the wilderness and we live that out for the rest of our lives.

A LINE OF COMMUNICATION
The first part of the word communication is commune. In the wilderness, we commune with God in the wonderful way He speaks to us.

We learn to love and respect what God says to us in the wilderness. This is the place where we first get a great value for His word.

Again, the lessons we learn in the wilderness become core values in our lives as we go into the Promised Land. These core values and principles are what keep us close to God as He gets ready to bless our socks off.

He wants us just as dependent on him in the land flowing with milk and honey as we are in the land of desolation. He wants us to welcome His presence and His word as we build His Kingdom and displace His enemies in the place He is leading us to be more than conquerors.

SCHOOL OF HARD KNOCKS

The Lessons of the wilderness teach us who God is to us and who we are to Him.

We learn to be completely dependent on His presence.

We learn to be completely dependent upon His word.

We learn to stay close to His manifest presence.

We learn that whatever the problem is in our lives, God is not the problem.

We learn to worship Him no matter what the day brings us.

We learn to look at God instead of our harsh circumstances and to let His presence dictate the environment we live in instead of anything else.

We learn to be ok with unexplainable things and supernatural experiences.

We learn to value His voice and His manifest presence more than anything else.

We learn to stay separate not to fall prey to the frenzy of the mob.

We learn to march at the beat of His drum and live with His light in a place that is dark to everyone else.

We learn that God is really really good and that it is really really good to know God.

We learn these things through personal experience with Him in this place called wilderness. What we learn of God becomes our personal testimony of Him and our testimony makes us overcomers as we move /forward from here.

And they overcame him by the blood of the Lamb, and by the word of their testimony; and they loved not their lives unto death. Revelation 12:11

So if you are going to get your upgrade and go to the next level, you cannot rebel against God in your wilderness experience.

You run to Him.

How you act determines if you spend 40 days like Jesus did or 40 years like Moses. It is really up to you.

It is so important we learn to live and be happy in God's presence because in the wilderness, the battle is about survival but in the Promised Land it is all about advancing!

The enemy of dreaming is surviving. God wants you to get through your wilderness so that you can get past surviving. The enemy must be displaced from the places God has given you as an inheritance and it is in Gods amazing presence, in the wilderness, where He changes us from helpless slaves to overcoming warriors.

So instead of learning how to protect yourself, God wants to teach you how to fight. The next section will be on these principles.

WHAT IF?
What if you didn't need a disaster to run to the presence of God? What if right now you began to thirst after a powerful, intimate experience with God.

What if you and I right now cranked up the value we have for hearing God speak.

What if we let our experience with God, during the tough times we have already gone through, teach us that in Jesus Christ, we have life and we will never find it anywhere else.

What if we put our complete dependency on Him right now, no matter how blessed we are. What if we were just as desperate for Him and worshiped him right this second as in any time we were devastated by terrible circumstances.

I'll tell you what. The power and manifest presence of God would show up the same way in our promised land as He does in the wilderness, only it would be better because the whole thing was initiated by our longing for Him instead of a painful circumstance.

If you and I could manage that, I promise you there would be prayers answered we have never seen and supernatural breakthrough we have never experienced.

PRAYERS WE LEARNED IN THE WILDERNESS

Where ever you are at, I encourage you to take a moment, worship King Jesus and set you heart in a place like this.

"Jesus I want to be alone with you. God you are my life and there is no life apart from you. I am in desperate need of you, right now, right this second. You are my God and there is no other.

I love how supernatural and unlimited you are. I love how you speak to me, command me, encourage me, protect me, lead me, feed me, provide for me and love me.

I am not a self-made person. All that I have comes from you. All that I am comes from you. All that I put my hand to comes from you. I don't want to do anything apart from you. I don't want to give my heart to anybody else. I belong to you and you to me. I know it is You Who has saved me.

You taught me these things in the wilderness. You were so good to me in my terrible wilderness and I love you for that. I will not forget you in my abundance. I will not say I'm too busy when you call me in my blessed place. I am yours and you are mine. You taught me that in the wilderness and I will not forget.

I love you Jesus."

_____

Put your name here.

GOD THOUGHTS AND MEDITATIONS
SUMMARY OF THE LESSONS OF THE WILDERNESS

_____

_____

_____

_____

_____

_____

_____

_____

_____

_____

The wilderness is not meant to be permanent for us but its lessons should be.

Some of the things we learn in our wilderness experience that we can never ever forget if we want to continue /forward are...

God is good.
He is our friend and the world is not our friend

God loves my personal and intimate company with Him. He gets Jealous when I give my heart to anything other than Him.

God loves to be alone with me.

I am not a victim and not a slave but an overcoming warrior and child of the King. He has made me that.

I will live with a huge value for God's manifest presence in my life and set up my "camp" based on His presence.

I will live with a huge value for His word both written and spoken.

I understand that God does things supernaturally and I do not have to have an explanation for everything.

I have no life outside of Him. Period.

When God moves, I move so I must be constantly watching for how He wants to lead me.

I am learning a new culture based on how God does things instead of how everybody else does things.

I do not need a committee; I need to believe what He says. No matter how dangerous or outrageous.

When I learn these things, and when these things become core values in my life, I graduate and get my upgrade. Case closed.

Psalm 63:1-11
A Psalm of David, when he was in the wilderness of Judah. O God, you are my God; earnestly I seek you; my soul thirsts for you; my flesh faints for you, as in a dry and weary land where there is no water. So I have looked upon you in the sanctuary, beholding your power and glory. Because your steadfast love is better than life, my lips will praise you. So I will bless you as long as I live; in your name I will lift up my hands. My soul will be satisfied as with fat and rich food, and my mouth will praise you with joyful lips,...

SECTION FOUR
Equipped For Your Journey

Fatty Rossiter: It was already loaded. Clyde, you have three pistols and you only have one arm for Pete's sake.
Clyde: Well I just don't want to be killed for lack of shootin' back.

UNFORGIVEN 1992

CHAPTER ELEVEN

Skill sets and values for the Next Level

The spirit of Saint Louis is not just the airplane hanging in the Smithsonian institute. It's a very real heart set of a people group from Missouri who equipped adventurous people for their journey west from there.

The giant arch on the river in Saint Louis stands as the symbol for the city. The gateway to the west.

For a longtime, if you were adventurous enough to head out west, Saint Louis was the place you went to get equipped for the journey.

The Frontier was actually doable but only if you had the right equipment. And so it is with your journey into your next level so make sure your bags are packed right.

ACHIEVING GOALS & FULFILLING VISION

This is going to be one of those Jewels in this book that can really change everything if you take it seriously. It's simple but so powerful.

If you are going to move /forward and get your upgrade you must become skilled at achieving goals. I pray for it, I meditate on it and pursue supernatural skill sets for getting things done. A very simple discipline I follow has helped me master skills in achieving goals in areas of my life. There are four steps to this and this is what they look like.

(1) SET ACHIEVABLE GOALS
This is all about Vision.

Do a word study on Vision and let the Holy Spirit lead you to whole new places of revelation and invitation in what it means to be a visionary in every part of your life.

(2) PUT TOGETHER A STRATEGY AND A PLAN. This is all about Sound Counsel.

Do a word study on counsel and let the Holy Spirit lead you to whole new places of revelation and invitation in what it means to seek out and find your own Godly counsel on how to do things that you don't know how to do. You must be a teachable person to really be smart.

(3) TAKE ACTION
This is all about Courage.
Do a word study on courage and learn everything you can on the subject of courage. Let the Holy Spirit lead you in what it means to have courage and to take action when the time is required.

(4) REVIEW AND STAY ON TRACK
This is all about meditation and contemplation. You have got to know how to think God thoughts and practice stillness. Your times of reflection and review need to be clear and full of the peace that comes from when Jesus is on His throne. Do a word study on meditation and let the Holy Spirit lead you to whole new places of revelation and invitation in what it means to think like he thinks on whatever subject you need to agree with Him on.

If you were to take these four steps seriously, I can tell you from personal experience, you would become skilled at achieving goals. That makes you a world changer!

Maybe this a good time for you to write these four steps down and begin a journey of taking on hell with a water pistol.

There are things you can do that none of the rest of us can, so go do it! Partner with the Holy Spirit, put together a strategic counsel to plan it out, make a team of go getters to get it done and dedicate your life to a life of contemplation and making sure you constantly retune.

VALUES, PRINCIPLES & PRIORITIES
Your value for self-preservation is actually the enemy of your upgrade. Your need to survive is in direct contrast to your need to live.

If you have a huge value for survival you will never move /forward. Your fear of failure has to be dealt with. We must have a higher value for living life than protecting our lives.

Jesus put it this way,
And he said unto his disciples, Therefore I say unto you, Take no thought for your life, what you shall eat; neither for the body, what you shall put on
Luke 12:22

He is not saying don't make a plan or don't take responsibility for your life. He is saying do not live your life as a survivor!

We have to have a higher value for overcoming than a value for surviving! You are not called to survive, you are called to overcome.

SNOWY DAY BATTLES
In the book of 2nd Samuel, the bible talks about the exploits of a warrior who hung out with David.

Benaiah son of Jehoiada was a valiant fighter from Kabzeel, who performed great exploits. He struck down two of Moab's best men. He also went down into a pit on a snowy day and killed a lion. 2 Samuel 23:20

This guy was not the kind of guy who ran for comfort when it was cold outside nor was he the kind of person who could pass up a pit with a lion in it. He had to Jump in.

What kind of priorities does a man have to have to look down into a pit where a lion is trapped and say, "I am jumping in!" Survival and comfort were obviously not at the top of his list. He had a greater interest in overcoming incredible odds than anything else and the bible says this man...*"performed great exploits."*

He far outranked and went past other people around him because he was not there to try and survive, he was there to live at a higher level.

THERE IS A DIFFERENCE
The difference between a survivor and an overcomer is the difference between the wilderness and the Promised Land. A survivor is someone who suffers a terrible attack and lives to tell about it. I want to tell you that in the Kingdom, this is not always good enough.

An overcomer is someone who suffers terrible attack, rises up and kills the attacker.

Survivors are victimized.
Overcomers are victorious.

Survivors have wounds
Overcomers have scars (like Jesus)

Survivors are Peace keepers
(Like the United Nation Peace Keeping Force, basically worthless in my estimation, if you don't believe me ask a Rwandan.)
Overcomers are Peace Makers
(Like the pistol that Samuel Colt made and the sons of God Jesus refers to in Matthew 5:9)

Survivors go through the fire and live life in constant reference to how they have been burned.
Overcomers go through the fire and don't even have the smell of smoke on their clothes.

There is a big difference between survivors and overcomers and another major difference is that survivors don't inherit the promises. -Overcomers do.

Promised Land Living
There are 17 promises reserved for overcomers in the book of Revelation. I want to take a look at them.

1. Revelation 2:7 says *"To him that overcometh will I give to eat of the tree of life, which is in the midst of the paradise of God."*

This is all about having eternal life and redemption from what Adam and Eve were originally thrown out of. Total restoration with God is the way it is supposed to be where we taste and see that the Lord is good.

2. Revelation 2:11 says *"He that overcometh shall not be hurt of the second death"*

The overcomer doesn't have to worry about being separated from God ever again. We will be in His presence and in His presence is the fullness of joy.

3. Revelation 2:17 says *"To him that overcometh will I give to eat of the hidden manna."*

Jesus is the hidden manna. The Bible says in John 6: 32 – 33 "Then Jesus said unto them, Verily, verily, I say unto you, Moses gave you not that bread from heaven; but my Father giveth you the true bread from heaven. For the bread of God is he which cometh down from heaven, and giveth life unto the world." Jesus is the hidden manna.

4. Revelation 2:17 says *"and will give him a white stone,"*

This is the promise of acquittal. It refers back to when a person was tried for a crime the judge would hear the case and make their decision by giving either a white stone which said the person was innocent or a black stone which stated that the person was guilty. God promises an overcomer a white stone meaning that He says you are not found guilty.

The promise of admittance: This also refers back to times past when a person tried to get into a certain organization the members of the organization would cast a secret vote whether or not to accept them into their organization. They would place either a white stone or a black stone in the box and if the stones were all white the person was accepted into the organization. However if the stone was black it said that the person had not been accepted. When you get the white stone, God says, "You are in!"

5. Revelation 2:17 says *"and in the stone a new name written, which no man knoweth saving he that receiveth it."* Let's continue.

6.Revelation 2:26 says "And he that overcometh, and keepeth my works unto the end, to him will I give power over the nations"

7. Revelation 3:5 says *"He that overcometh, the same shall be clothed in white raiment"*

8. Revelation 3:5 says *"and I will not blot out his name out of the book of life"*

9. Revelation 3:5 says *"but I will confess his name before my Father, and before his angels."*

10. Revelation 3:12 says *"Him that overcometh will I make a pillar in the temple of my God"*

11. Revelation 3:12 *"and I will write upon him the name of my God"*

12. Revelation 3:12 *"and the name of the city of my God, [which is] new Jerusalem,"*

12. Revelation 3:12 *"and the name of the city of my God, [which is] new Jerusalem,"* (The promise of the specific identity of new Jerusalem)

14. Revelation 3:21 "To him that overcometh will I grant to sit with me in my throne, even as I also overcame, and am set down with my Father in his throne"

15. Revelation 21:7 *"He that overcometh shall inherit all things;"*

16. Revelation 21:7 *"and I will be his God"*

17. Revelation 21:7 *"and he shall be my son."*

PUT ON YOUR NIKE

What is an overcomer? The Greek word "Nikao" means one that prevails, conquers, and gets the victory over. It is to surmount difficulties. It is the word the Company NIKE named their shoes after.

So when we say we are overcomers we are saying we strive to prevail and stomp on the difficulties which come our way. We strive to uproot, unhinge and displace the enemy where ever we encounter it.

We have a huge value for this as overcomers. We love it when God wins and gets the victory. We live dedicated to seeing Heaven invade earth.

John says in 1 John 5:4 *"Whatsoever is born of God overcometh the world."*

If you are born of God you must remove any notion of an option to overcome. Benaiah son of Jehoiada jumped down into that pit and took on a lion because he had no option to walk past it. He overcame it and we are still talking about it 3000 years later.

You are going to have to decide that you are going to conform your life to look more like an overcomer than a survivor.

"Be not overcome of evil, but overcome evil with good." Rom. 12:21.

GREAT BIG VALUES
The family Values in this family that you and I are a part of come from the heart of the Father Himself. We learn to make a big deal out of what He makes a big deal out of and as we MAGNIFY the Lord it becomes clear what we should blow up and dial down.

There are lots of Godly people who never master the art of upgrade or get the fever for /forward. That's not you.

So since you are different it stands to reason that you are going to make a big deal out of things that others do not. I have found that the values of those of us who journey in the fast lane are quite a bit different.

Do you remember the lessons of the Wilderness?

When you learn the lesson, you learn to continue to have a high priority for the thing you have been taught. Some of the values appreciated by people who move /forward look like this.

VALUES FOR /FORWARD LIVING PEOPLE

The Presence Of God : Personal Encounter
We highly value complete dependency on His manifest presence because in His presence we grow and change and find and live life. We make a big deal out of seeking Him and finding Him in both new and familiar ways. We want Him in every single part of our Life and we want to know what He thinks because we want to be in agreement with Him. We don't care how God shows up as long as He shows up. We value Manifest presence and intimacy over omnipresence and we know He is going to change us every single time we experience Him in a whole new way.

We learn to stay close to His presence then we learn how to carry His presence. Living in the presence of God and knowing by experience He is with us constantly, gives us the courage to stomp in uncharted territory and upon the necks of opposing enemies. If we want to live /forward, we cannot have too high of a value for ongoing experience in the presence of God.

The Word Of God : Personal Communication
We have a huge Value for His word both spoken and written. We love hearing Him speak to us. We get super excited when God

reveals something new to us. Those of us who live life /forward constantly look for the heart of God in everything around. We are dedicated to asking, seeking and knocking and we do all that we can to keep our passion high for God's voice in our life.

We do not take the voice of God for granted and we remain totally dependent upon Him as hearers knowing these certain truths.

Just because God is speaking doesn't mean that we know it so we must be listening.

Just because we know God is speaking does not mean we understand what God is saying so we must be dependent upon Him for the interpretation.

Just because we understand it does not mean we know what to do with it so we must be dependent on His guidance.

We have a huge value for hearing God speak because we choose relationship over anything and because with a word from God comes authority to accomplish anything.

Mystery and waiting; as much as Strategy and Decisive Action.

At the same time we are held responsible for partnering with Him in planning and in making strategic moves, we are also held responsible for waiting on Him in things we don't even know how to articulate. We have a huge value for the well-articulated and crafted out word God gives us in the areas He has caused us to master. We also have a huge Value for daring to step into the unknown. Because of our enormous value for progression and upgrade we have learned to celebrate the joy of discovery. We do not have to have an explanation for everything when Jesus is the answer to everything.

Supernatural Experience

Those of us who truly live life /forward do so knowing that nothing is impossible because of Jesus Christ. It is perfectly natural for us to live supernatural lives and we refuse to consider any other notion.

THE CHIEF ARCHITECT

Several years ago I spent a year of my life mapping out what the main values of our Leadership team should be because I believe that Values define the team.

As the Pastor of OpenDoor Church I don't think my most important job is to be the best preacher around, which I am hands down for at least a 100 mile radius. I think my main job is to be the architect of the culture of the house.

To make sure that the way we do things and relate to each other looks more like heaven than earth on any given day of the week. It is not something we always accomplish but it is something we always go after and it's what we make a big deal out of -or don't make a big deal out of, that defines how and what we do. The how and what we do is our culture and if it is toxic, it doesn't matter at all if we preach the bible and have a salvation call every Sunday.

I don't think God moves through a church service, I think God moves through the relationships of the people within the church services.

So not only do values define team but values also define culture.

Clear Definition

Have you ever really mapped out the things you are determined to highly value? If not let me tell you where to start. You start by determining you are going to make a big deal out of what God makes a big deal out of. You are going to line up your heart with God's heart.

From that place you begin to map out your own values with your own unique destination and purpose.

Eliminate the things that don't fit. Chisel away the things that don't look like God's plan for your life. Turn up the fire and crank up the volume on the areas that must be staples for your /forward life living.

Just list the highest values you have to have for your heart to look like His heart and for your life to look like the one He is inviting you into. Maybe it's just good to write down single word "headlines" at first, like; Supernatural, dreaming, forgiving, etc. and then come back and ask the Holy Spirit to help you articulate a well-crafted and more articulate definition of your core value.

For instance, maybe your "Supernatural" headline may turn into a statement like the one that follows.

I value the supernatural side of God and me because I choose not to live a powerless life.

Or

I have a high value for living a naturally supernatural life believing that because Jesus is risen from the dead, absolutely nothing is impossible.

Your "Forgiving" headline may turn into a language that changes everything for you.

I Value, celebrate, encourage and practice forgiveness knowing God values restoration over punishment.

Pen some of those *headlines* or *articles* of spirit led core values here and know this is a work in progress.

_____

_____

_____

_____

_____

_____

_____

_____

_____

_____

_____

_____

_____

_____

_____

_____

_____

_____

_____

_____

John says in 1 John 5:4 *"Whatsoever is born of God overcometh the world."*

"If you are born of God you must remove any notion of any option to overcome."
Troy Brewer : Living Life /Forward

CHAPTER TWELVE

Your Big Finish /Forward.

In getting ready to finish this book, I want to talk to you about the subject of how you are going to finish.

You do know there is a big finish coming, right?

See the hope and future that God gives us in fact, an expected end. That's why Jeremiah 29:11 is sometimes translated as *hope* and sometimes as *expected end.*

For I know the plans I have for you," declares the Lord, "plans to prosper you and not to harm you, plans to give you hope and a future" NIV

For I know the thoughts that I think toward you, saith the Lord, thoughts of peace, and not of evil, to give you an expected end KJV

God wants you to expect and have great hope for where your life will end up and when you start thinking about that, you start thinking about the legacy you leave behind you.

THE BOURNE LEGACY

You were born not just to make it but to make a way for others to make it. All of this /forward living is not just about you. Promised land living is a constant awareness of destiny, legacy and leaving a heritage of /forward momentum for others to build on and follow behind. Like Jesus, we have become builders and carpenters.

We have to contemplate and chew on this notion, years before we get there.

Alfred Allen once said "It is easier to fight for one's principles than to live up to them." and one day your life is going to require that you have lived up to what you have fought so hard for.

You are going to fight and push and run and overcome and build and achieve and declare and pursue and someday, someday not too very long from this very moment, you will finish your race.

Now don't start freaking out, you need to know how this works. For you to walk in the power of God, He requires you to live in the paradox of complete awareness of your eternity and your short time here.

Neither should surprise you.

When you get ready for your big finish, I hope like Paul, that you will be able to look back at your fight for /forward and say, "Man, I fought a good fight."

For I am already being poured out like a drink offering, and the time for my departure is near. I have fought the good fight, I have finished the race, I have kept the faith. Now there is in store for me the crown of righteousness, which the Lord, the righteous Judge, will award to me on that day—and not only to me, but also to all who have longed for his appearing. 2 Tim 4:6-8

Take a look at this very familiar place in the bible.

Notice How Paul was thinking not only about himself, at the end of his life, but for *all who long for the appearing of Jesus.*

Now notice that Paul fought a good fight and a good fight is one that you win.

Once your head has really gone there, let it sink in that this text is all about Paul's big finish.

Paul finished well. Paul knew his finish was a good one before he died.

Not everybody can say that. Paul could say it with confidence because it had been his intention for decades before. He worked hard towards it and he reaped what he sowed. He was determined to finish well way before he finished.

Thirteen years before his big finish, Paul wrote these words to his friends at Corinth and I paraphrase.

I am serious about finishing well in my Christian ministry. I discipline myself for fear that after challenging others into the Christian life I myself might become a casualty. 1Cor 9:24-27 PTV

Paul was like, "Look, I'm not going to be a world changer and then collapse at the end of this thing."

He actually disciplined Himself towards a predetermined big finish. When Paul lived life /forward it wasn't just to get to heaven, it was to bring heaven to earth and he wanted a grand finale.

CASUALTIES OF WAR
America has seen its share of war casualties.
25,000 in the revolutionary war; 212,938 in the Civil war; 291,557 just in the 2nd world war, but there have been millions of Christians who were strong in the Lord for short seasons and were overwhelmed before the war was over.

Paul said he didn't want to become a casualty. He decided he would be a key player at the end of his life. We might think of this in terms of people losing their faith but a lot of really Godly people only do exploits for the Lord in very short times of their lives.

Those people, who do great things then burn out, might make a valuable contribution in the kingdom but not in terms of legacy. Someone else has to do that for them. Someone who was determined to finish well.

This reminds me of a letter one of my heroes wrote as he penned his very last letter from behind the adobe walls of the Alamo.

"Take care of my little boy. If the country should be saved, I may make him a splendid fortune; but if the country should be lost, and I should perish, he will have nothing but the proud recollection that he is the son of a man who died for his country." William Barrett Travis, Commander of the Alamo and defender of Texas Freedom. 1836

Travis understood this principle. He knew that no matter how hard they fought, his /forward legacy depended on him finishing well.

What Travis was not able to accomplish at the Alamo, another warrior by the name of Houston was able to finish at San Jacinto. -And He finished it well.

TALE OF TWO WARRIORS
Two of the greatest warriors the world has ever seen are revealed to the world through the bible and known to all of us as Samson and David.

The Book of Judges tells us that among Samson's exploits, he tore a lion apart with his bare hands (14:6), struck down 30 Philistine men (14:20), caught 300 foxes and tied their tails together (15:4), slaughtered 1,000 men with a donkey's jawbone (15:15), tore off the city gate of Gaza and carried it to the top of a hill (16:3), and finally, he pushed down the pillar holding up the Philistine temple, killing 3,000 people (16:30).

Several books in the Old Testament tell us about this amazing man David.

Who has not heard of the teenager who played head on collision with a giant from Gath and won the day? You do realize he cut his head off with the monster's own sword?

David's first action as king was to capture what is now the City of David in Jerusalem, fortify it and build himself a palace. When the Philistines heard that David had been anointed king and was threatening their hegemony over all of Palestine, they attacked, spread out over the Valley of Raphaim and captured Bethlehem. David retaliated and, in three battles, forced the Philistines out of Israel. This was his first action as King.

David then began fighting wars against Israel's neighbors on the east bank of the Jordan. He defeated the Moabites, the Edomites, the Ammonites and the Arameans. These wars began as defensive wars, but ended with the establishment of his mighty empire that extended over both sides of the Jordan River, as far as the Mediterranean Sea.

David fought monsters as a child and even on his deathbed, as a feeble old man, he was still killing Israel's enemies.

BEYOND COMPARE
Both of these guys are so similar in so many ways. Consider some of these examples.

Both of them were supernaturally anointed for warfare.

Both fought lions as young men.

Both of them were poets.

Both of them were passionate lovers.

Both of them were fearless.

Both of them were renowned.

Both of them were commissioned by God to deal with the Philistines.

Both of them are listed in Hebrews 11 as being in the great *hall of fame* of faith.

Samson and David were both supernatural rock stars of their day and warrior poets who blew everyone's mind. Yet, even though they were so similar, there really is no comparison to these two. In fact, you may never have seen any biblical comparison between Samson and David until now. You don't compare Samson and David even though they are so similar in so many ways. Do you know why?

Because there is no comparison at all when it comes to the legacy and the heritage they left.

Great exploits and living /forward only matter to everyone else if it leaves a great legacy.

The only legacy and heritage Samson left us was nearly 400 years of additional slavery from the philistines because he could not finish well.

It took David to rise up and do exploits that freed the nation and brought justice to the land. That was never going to happen from the likes of Samson.

You may have heard it preached that he did and a lot of people think he finished well because of how he died. This is how the bible puts it.

Samson said, "Let me die with the Philistines!" Then he pushed with all his might, and down came the temple on the rulers and all the people in it. Thus he killed many more when he died than while he lived Judges 16:30

Let me humbly say that as much as I love Samson, It is never a good thing when your nation is better off with you dead, then when you were alive. Samson was better off when he was alive but the nation of Israel wasn't. That's not good.

Samson was so out of control. He was so out of tune with his great purpose and so stuck on himself, his last prayer, and this is in a great state of humility for him, mentions me, I and mine, no less than 7 times.

28 Then Samson called to the Lord, saying, "O Lord God, remember me, I pray! Strengthen me, I pray, just this once, O God, that I may with one blow take vengeance on the Philistines for my two eyes!" 29 And Samson took hold of the two middle pillars which supported the temple, and he braced himself against them, one on his right and the other on his left. 30 Then Samson said, "Let me die with the Philistines!" And he pushed with all his might, and the temple fell on the lords and all the people who were in it. So the dead that he killed at his death were more than he had killed in his life.
Judges 16 NKJV

A bad ending to a really good movie tends to ruin the whole show. It definitely ruins the legacy when this is a life anointed of the Lord.

See to finish "well", you have to finish some things. There are some things that should not be there after you are there. -And that could never be said of Samson.

The Philistines still ruled and enslaved and caused great torment long after Samson. There was another 400 years of unnecessary terrible hardship - that is until David showed up. He started something that David would have to finish.

Even the angel of the Lord, in announcing Samson's miraculous birth, knew he would do exploits but not finish well.

"...for the child shall be a Nazirite to God from the womb; and he shall begin to deliver Israel out of the hand of the Philistines." Judges 13:5 NKJV

On the Contrary, David's exploits of war left his son Solomon 40 years of peace and left every Christian the actual Prince of Peace Himself. Jesus Christ is the greatest legacy of David. (Matthew 1:17)

All of us will forever be grateful because David was a man who didn't just do great things for a season, but He finished really really well.

TRAITS OF A GREAT /FORWARD FINISHER

One of the greatest recent contributors to the body of Christ, in theological study, in my opinion, is a guy by the name of J Robert Clinton.

As Senior Professor of Leadership at Fuller Theological Seminary, his famous study on leaders who finish well has become known throughout the world as a ground breaking revelation.

In his widely published free download he says,

"There are around 800 or so leaders mentioned in the Bible. There are about 100 who have data that helps you interpret their leadership. About 50 of these have enough data for evaluation of their finish. About 1 in 3 finished well. Anecdotal evidence from today indicates that this ratio is probably generous. Probably less than 1 in 3 are finishing well today."

He goes on to list the major reasons why a lot of great people do not finish in a great way and then he lists why the minority does actually finish well.

He said, *"At the time of this article I have studied nearly 1300 cases with about 50 Bible leaders, perhaps 100 historical leaders and the rest contemporary leaders. The findings for enhancements and barriers generally hold true.*

And what is true of Biblical leaders is equally true of historical and contemporary leaders.

The Six Characteristics of Leaders who Finish Well according to Dr. Clinton look like this.

Characteristic 1 - They maintain a personal vibrant relationship with God right up to the end.

Characteristic 2 - They maintain a learning posture and can learn from various kinds of sources—life especially.

Characteristic 3 - They manifest Christ-likeness in character as evidenced by the fruit of the Spirit in their lives.

Characteristic 4 - Truth is lived out in their lives so that convictions and promises of God are seen to be real.

Characteristic 5 - They leave behind one or more ultimate contributions.

Characteristic 6 - They walk with a growing awareness of a sense of destiny and see some or all of it fulfilled.

Yeah so people don't just finish well. They Finish well because like, Paul said, they discipline themselves so that they don't become casualties.

Our Brother from Fuller has found at least six of those traits and we would do well to forge them into our personalities, if they are not already there.

PROPHETIC PARTNERSHIP

So this book ends with the end of the book of John. Jesus and Peter are walking near the great Israeli Lake called Galilee and they are having this amazing discussion.

I love the end of the book of John because we actually get to listen in on this very personal conversation between the resurrected hero of the universe and one of the recently restored heroes of the fledgling church.

Jesus is asking him this same question over and over again and Peter begins to wonder what He should know that the Lord only knows.

...and Peter was grieved because He said to him the third time, "Do you love Me?"And he said to Him, "Lord, You know all things; You know that I love You." Jesus said to him, "Feed My sheep. John 21:17

Now everybody preaches on the beauty of that message but all the sudden Jesus turns to Peter and says, "Let me tell you something else I know..."
and where this conversation goes from here is just outright glorious.

Most assuredly, I say to you, when you were younger, you girded yourself and walked where you wished; but when you are old, you will stretch out your hands, and another will gird you and carry you where you do not wish." 19 This He spoke, signifying by what death he would glorify God. And when He had spoken this, He said to him, "Follow Me." John 21: 18 & 19

Did you catch it? Jesus turns to Peter and I bet it was with a smile, He says, "You are going to finish really well."

... This He spoke, signifying by what death he would glorify God...

Peter had a history of being unpredictable when he got overwhelmed. Peter, world famous by now for denying Jesus 3 times and cussing like the sailor he was, was personally encouraged by Jesus Himself on how his big finish /forward would go.

"...Peter, You are going to go places you never would have gone before. I know how you are going to finish and it's all going to glorify me..."

I bet if you listen closely you would hear him tell you the same thing. I bet if you would walk close to Jesus, separate from the crowds, letting him deal with you however he really wanted to, I bet you he will say something LIKE, "Oh listen, I've seen how you finish and it's just plain glorious!"

I would bet snow white's seven character password on it.

EXIT THE WARRIOR

Like today's Tom Sawyer, you are ready for your next big adventure and Just like Mark Twain's masterpiece, Yours will be a great ending.

"But I reckon I got to light out for the Territory ahead of the rest, because Aunt Sally she's going to adopt me and sivilize me and I can't stand it. I been there before."
Last line from the adventures of Huckleberry Finn.

The Bible calls you a Living Epistle (2 Corinthians 3:2)

This means a walking book being written by God and before your last Chapter has finished into the grand masterpiece that blows everyone's mind when they read it, You will already know how it's going to end.

-With great Victory.

Your story is not a sad one but a glorious one and you seal the deal by finishing well.

God Bless you in your journey /forward. May the Life you live continue to look more like your Destiny than your History. When you finally finish accomplishing vision, killing giants, slaying dragons and mapping it out for others behind you, look for me in that incredible place with the most Amazing person in the universe. Everything /forward from here is found in Jesus. I will see you on the great day and we will celebrate together.

GOD THOUGHTS AND MEDITATIONS
HOW WILL YOU FINISH WELL?

_____

_____

_____

_____

_____

_____

_____

For I know the thoughts that I think toward you, saith the Lord, thoughts of peace, and not of evil, to give you an expected end KJV

You are going to fight and push and run and overcome and build and achieve and declare and pursue and someday, someday not too very long from this very moment, you will finish your race.

For you to walk in the power of God, He requires you to live in the paradox of complete awareness of your eternity and your short time here.

Troy Brewer : Living Life /Forward

Bibliography

It is important to note that I do not endorse all of the content that is in these books and especially these web sites. It is also important to note that they do not endorse the content in my book either. Some of these sites are not even Christian in content but are Historic or mathematic sites. Below are the links and the information relevant to the information contained in this book.

Web Site Links

Information on Dr. J Robert Clinton

www.gerryrunn.com
The J Robert Clinton archives

Fuller University on Professor Clinton
http://www.fuller.edu/academics/faculty/robert-clinton.aspx

Fast facts on numbers

http://www.wordworx.co.nz/panin.html
Ivan Panin discoveries

http://christianbeliefs.org/articles/biblenumerics.html
Criticism of Panin and bible numeric

http://www.datesinhistory.com
Dates in History

www.carm.org/questions/numbers.htm
Additional number in scripture site

http://www.christiananswers.net/q-wall/wal-g011.html
George Washington

http://www.ku.edu/carrie/docs/amdocs_index.html
Documents for the study of American History

www.Historybuff.com
Bonnie & Clyde information

Casualties of war statistics
http://en.wikipedia.org/wiki/United_States_military_
casualties_of_war

www.teachinghearts.org/dre17httnumber.html
Timeslines, Bible and numbers in scripture.

www.thebelieversorganization.org
Experts on the King James Bible

www.carm.org
Christian Apologetics and Research Ministry

www.jewishpath.org
Hebrew Gematria studies

www.stevenjcamp.blogspot.com
"CAMPONTHIS" incredible Web site OF Steve Camp

www.historychannel.com/today
This day in History

www.brainyhistory.com

Geography, dictionary, encyclopedia, this day in History and more

www.bibarch.com
Biblical archeology site

www.answeres.com/topic/double-entendre
Double-entendre examples and dictionary.

Sermons & Teachers as contributories

Finishing Well—Six Characteristics
By Dr. J. Robert Clinton

The 17 promises given to the overcomer
Pastor Melvin Maughmer, JR.

The 34 Pre-resurrection miracles of Christ
Hampton Keathley IV, Th.M. 1995 graduate of Dallas Theological Seminary

Pastor David Crone
The Mission, Vacaville, California

Pastor Howard Richardson
Gates of Glory Church Dallas, Texas

Pastor Jim Maxwell
Ft Worth, Texas

Pastor Gene Izzaguira
Mission Divina, Brownsville Texas

Pastor Steve Fish
Convergence Church, Ft Worth Texas

BOOKS

I highly recommend these books for any bible thumper. I must note one more time my endorsement of their book does not mean that they endorse mine.

The Power of your Life message.
David Crone. published by Destiny image publishers
www.davecrone.com

Number in scripture
E.W Bullinger
Kregal publications
Grand Rapids MI 49501

A Divine Confrontation
Graham Cooke
Destiny Image Publishing, 1999
also see Brilliant Bookhouse

The Next Level
(What insiders know about executive success)
By Scott Eblin
Nicolas Brealey Publishing

Very helpful search engines I used in my research

http://www.biblegateway.com
The main search engine I use to look up bible passages

http://www.crosssearch.com/

http://www.gospelcom.net/

http://wikipedia.org/
Amazing free encyclopedia

http://dictionary.com

http://www.datesinhistory.com

www.Bible-Topics.com
This website includes almost 700 topics. Excellent study tool.

Thank You

Debbie and Richmond Caldwell
Debbie, your help in editing and working with this book was timed completely by the Holy Spirit. Thank you so much.

Richmond, when you offered to send Leanna and I with you to invade your vacation, I knew that I would have a week to finish this book. Thank you so much for your personal friendship and know that God used your blessing to help me wrap this work up in a way I hope will benefit others.

William Edward Brewer
Dad, I started this book in the stormiest and most difficult time of my life, determined to get out of the mess that was trying to kill me. Thank you for standing with me, loving me and helping me through that dark and dreadful year.

Seeing how you loved me, and stood for me in 2011 caused me to see my Heavenly Father standing with me and loving me. 2012 was amazing and now 2013 is ten levels higher in every way because of who you are, sir.

Sure do love you, Pop.

About This Author

When Troy Brewer is not writing books, he is writing his widely published weekly newspaper column, Fresh from the Brewer.

He founded the OpenDoor Food bank in 95 and still works hard at giving away several million pounds of free food to over 26,000 people every year.

When he is not writing, he is singing love songs to his wife Leanna with one of his favorites from his growing collection of guitars.

Leanna is the Founding CEO of SPARK World Wide, an organization dedicated to Serving, Protecting And Raising Kids throughout the world. Troy serves on the board and teaches pastoral conferences for the regions at her sponsored orphanages in Uganda, Mexico, India and other places.
www.sparkworldwide.org

He can also be found teaching from the pulpit at OpenDoor Church in Joshua Texas, several times a week.
www.opendoorexperience.com

His weekly radio broadcast, *Experiencing Real Life*, can be heard on radio stations throughout the
United States and information can be found on his church website.

His four Kids Maegan, Benjamin, Luke and Rhema all live within a few miles from him and are building houses of their own.

Troy Brewer at the San Jacinto battle field.
Troy is a descendant of Henry Brewer who fought with Houston
for the freedom of Texas in 1836

Contact The Author

Email
troybrewer@me.com
Snail mail
PO Box 1349, Joshua TX 76058
Church Website
www.opendoorexperience.com
Spark Website
www.sparkworldwide.org
Facebook
www.facebook.com/troy.brewer.37

Troy speaks at a variety of conferences and churches, both
domestically and internationally. If you would like to inquire
into his availability for ministry, you can contact him through
the above information or call the offices at 817-645-6200

Other Books by this Author

Miracles With A Message
Aventine Press

Miracles with a message Is an amazing collection of modern day miracles interwoven with power packed, biblical wisdom that will build up your faith and encourage your heart. These chapters include, Miracle at Wedgewood: As a lunatic killer shot up a church in Ft Worth, Texas, the hand of God was leaving proof that He is still in the protecting business. Perfect Timing: A prisoner's prayer for a miracle caused God to deliver the very next day and of all places at The Ballpark In Arlington! Flight 191: On August 2, 1985 rescue workers frantically went through the wreckage of a crashed commercial airliner at DFW airport. Hours before that plane went down, God did an amazing miracle to keep a little girl from boarding that plane. These stories and many more will increase your faith, encourage your heart and advance your trust in the loving God we serve. These are not just Miracles; these are miracles with a message.

Soul Invasion
Aventine Press 2003

The battle for the brain is on and you can win this battle! It would be silly to think that God would want you to have victory throughout your life without winning the everyday battles between your two ears. If you are really serious about your walk with God, this sometimes funny, and sometimes somber group of tactics will

help you Sober up in correcting very real mental malfunctions.
SOUL INVASION will teach you effective Biblical strategies
including How to "armor up" in your thinking How to deal
with Haters How to Spiritually "arrest" your thoughts before
they progress & accelerate Jesus driven thinking that helps and
heals Confronting unhealthy mindsets in 11 common but very
different arenas and much much more! This Book will bring you
peace, and in knowing the Truth the Truth will set you free.

Fresh From The Brewer: Sips of Wisdom From the Carpenter's Cup
Aventine Press 2001-2003
Pastor Troy Brewer brings you a delightful
collection of his newspaper columns from
Johnson County, Texas. These incredible
stories & things observed come mixed
in his unique blend of powerful spiritual
insight, & witty southern charm. Wisdom
from the carpenter's cup was meant to be
slowly sipped on and then quickly acted
upon. Like a good cup of gourmet coffee
you have to savor it and cherish it until it
warms you like a thick blanket in the cold

of winter.   A timeless testament to the power of God's voice
through every day events, this collection is sure to encourage,
support, comfort and, most of all, inspire all readers for years
to come. This book is one cup that you won't want to put down.

Fresh From the Brewer Volume II: Sips of Wisdom From the Carpenter's Cup
Aventine Press 2004-2006
The second edition of witty and powerful insights from the pen of Troy Brewer is sure to encourage and inspire readers. Be refreshed by reading this companion issue and a timeless testament to the power of God's voice through every day events.

Numbers That Preach: Understanding God's Mathematical Lingo
Aventine Press 2007
Your Bible, your history books, and even your newspaper headlines are full of God shouting a powerful message of hope and healing. The same author who designed 24,900 miles around the planet, also calculated 24 hours around your clock, and predetermined 24 elders around the throne. But unless you know what God is consistently speaking through the number 24, you miss the message. In fact, you don't even know there is a message.

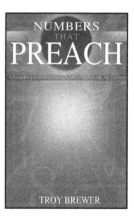

Numbers That Preach is a fun look at the otherwise hidden sermons God is declaring through His mathematical lingo. For more than twenty years, author Troy Brewer has studied Biblical text and collected interesting facts, figures and statistics that show powerful meaning in the numbers around us.

All of Troy's books can be found at Aventine press or online through Amazon and other fine book retailers.

CPSIA information can be obtained
at www.ICGtesting.com
Printed in the USA
LVHW032330090120
643191LV00017B/955/P